My Journey to Wholeness
with Bob and Mary Armstrong

My Journey to Wholeness

with Bob and Mary Armstrong

ANTHONY WILLEY

Tampa, Florida

The content associated with this book is the sole work and responsibility of the author. Gatekeeper Press had no involvement in the generation of this content.

My Journey to Wholeness with Bob and Mary Armstrong

Published by Gatekeeper Press
7853 Gunn Hwy., Suite 209
Tampa, FL 33626
www.GatekeeperPress.com

Copyright © 2024 by Anthony Willey

All rights reserved. Neither this book, nor any parts within it may be sold or reproduced in any form or by any electronic or mechanical means, including information storage and retrieval systems, without permission in writing from the author. The only exception is by a reviewer, who may quote short excerpts in a review.

Cover image: iStockphoto.com/fashayan (light pink budding rose plant)
Image on page 141: Icon of Saint John of San Francisco by Kimberly Mattson

Library of Congress Control Number: 2024936489

ISBN (hardcover): 9781662949173
eISBN: 9781662949203

FOREWORD
A Note of Thanks

No man is an island, so one man cannot write a book without a community behind him, at least not this one. I want to take a moment to thank several people who made this book possible.

First, I would like to thank God for the great gift of Bob and Mary Armstrong. I would not want to contemplate how my life would have been without them.

Next, I would like to thank John Goddard, who coached me with the kindness and truth in the writing of this book. I tend to be a surface writer, skipping over the surface of a smooth pond without examining what's below. John's council to go deeper is the reason this book has depth. John read through many rewrites of several manuscripts, and the gift of his advice and evidence of his kindness and generosity is the production of this book.

In addition to all of this he gave important background information and allowed me to view the scrapbook created for him by his mother.

Pictures were critical in providing context and allowed Bob and Mary to be seen in their younger years as well as adding faces to names.

I can never thank him enough for his contributions. Without them this work would have been a shallow and fleshless effort that would not do justice to these two dear people.

Jacob McGinnis was vital as well for this book's depth and breadth. He allowed me to use a project in school that he did when he was twelve called the Generations Project. Jacob and Bob wrote six letters to each other about their lives and interests. To my knowledge, this is the only example of a first-person account of Bob's life. It was a key piece in the timeline of the narrative. In addition, it came with pictures of his choice that illustrated his life. This allowed Bob to speak to us across time in his own words with images that he chose to share his life.

When I found I needed more pictures, Deacon Philip suggested that I talk to Jacob because he had access to pictures from the church archive that I could use. Jacob found them and then went the extra mile and talked to his mother Debbie, who shared wonderful pictures to add to the book.

I asked Jacob to write what the Armstrongs meant to him as he looked back from the perspective of a young man. His letter is moving and beautiful and speaks for all the godchildren and parishioners who knew and loved Bob and Mary.

I would like to thank John and Lynn Muheisen for the lovely lunch and conversation. It reminded me of the conversation with Bob and Mary. They also gave me several pictures, one of Mary and Bob together, which is one of my favorites, and one of Bob shortly after Mary passed, which shows him in the church he loved. In it he is being assisted by John, his godson after communion. One looks at Bob and one knows that his time to enter the Kingdom is close.

Father Jeremiah preached a magnificent homily about the woman with the issue of blood who touched Jesus. When I heard it, I knew that it would be among the final words in the book. It is perfect symmetry that this should be so. Bob and Mary observed Father Jeremiah's vocation from catechumen to priest in the last years of their lives. The sermon is a perfect summation of the love and need for God and His love for us. A story that Bob and Mary lived their whole lives.

I would like to thank my wife, dear Olga, for giving me the gift of time. She knew that I needed to go home to do the work of writing this piece. If I had not been given the month in Washington to complete it, I doubt the manuscript would have been completed. I owe her more than I can say.

If I had continued to work on this project alone it would have been a slow ponderous experience with shallow results. I believe that the Holy Spirit used the process of writing this book and seeking the help and support of others to teach me that any task is best served together, and the results always improved.

The entire month of November I felt like a pencil in the fingers of God. A theme running through this book is attributed to Miss Bacon's first-grade Sunday school teacher. **"If we listen, we can hear God's voice."** I was praying and trying to listen and hear Him.

Sentences and memories came day and night. I would write them down in my notebook. Invariably the words fit the narrative along with the letters and pictures, and together they presented the story of the Armstrongs' lives and my walk with them to the light of Christ's grace.

As I look at the finished work and reflect on how God's hand placed events and people in my life to bring me to the point of wholeness in Him, I begin to understand how He writes the stories of our lives to bring us to Him, the ultimate reality and joy of life.

Introduction

Robert and Mary Armstrong were a seemingly ordinary retired couple living in Marysville, Washington, and parishioners of Saint Paul the Apostle Orthodox Church. I was a struggling thirty-one-year-old man, searching for God, trying to live a life of faith and find a career.

Bob and Mary became my godparents upon my conversion to Orthodox Christianity in 1995. I soon discovered how extraordinary they were.

Their entire life was built upon an established foundation in Christ that suffering and the difficult challenges of life would not overcome them but be overcome by accepting them as God's providence for their salvation.

Through the embrace of their crosses of difficulties in relationships, personal setbacks, and exceptional losses. They experienced grace, wisdom, and blessing in overcoming them.

These crosses provided the path forward for them and others to a rich life of faith in Christ and a deep love for those they encountered. They found that no circumstance no matter how hard can overcome those with the love of Christ and those who live in Him.

Their faith thrived in all of life's joys and tragedies. Christ was the rock-solid foundation of their lives and theirs was a joyful resilient faith.

When Bob and Mary became my godparents, they took me into their lives, and for over twenty years, I observed how they prayed, their kind acts, how they worshipped during Holy Liturgy, their relationships with family, friends, parishioners, and godchildren. These were woven into the fabric of their lives and, as I grew closer, in mine as well.

I began to internalize and live this joyful resilient faith which was such a contrast to the one I had previously and in doing so changed.

Bob and Mary's faith and love drew me near to God and His grace and established within me a life of faith in Him. In this walk with Christ, I learned that every life lived in Him is extraordinary.

The intent of this book is to see and hear Bob and Mary in their writing, letters, books, pictures, interviews, and recollections of those who knew them.

Whenever possible pictures, memorabilia, interviews, quotations from books written by Mary, or about Mary, letters written by them or about them, and interviews, will be integrated within the narrative.

Mary did this beautifully with the books she authored and scrapbooks she created for her children and grandchildren to pass on her family's history to them.

This book is written in that spirit so that the legacy of Bob and Mary, their deep and abiding love for God and their joyful, resilient faith can be seen, heard, lived, and carried on by future generations. Let as now explore the life of two seemingly ordinary but truly extraordinary people.

———

When the sun's rays touch a rock, the rock begins to shine.
When a flame touches an unlit candle, it begins to burn.
When a magnet touches a metal object, the object becomes magnetized.
When an electric wire touches an ordinary wire, they both become electrified.
Father Jeremiah Vollman, Homily, October 29, 2023)

———

Psalm 138:11-12

If I say, "Surely the darkness will hide me
 and the light become night around me,"
[12] **even the darkness will not be dark to you;**
 the night will shine like the day,
 for darkness is as light to you.
[13] **For you created my inmost being;**
 you knit me together in my mother's womb.
[14] **I praise you because I am fearfully and wonderfully made.**

DARK BEFORE LIGHT
My Story

A pilgrimage is a journey with a purpose. Several years ago, my wife, son and I went on a journey to Israel to draw closer to Christ by walking in the places Christ walked and lived.

I have been on a pilgrimage to Christ and His light before I could articulate it. I felt that God was present in my life. There is no place to hide from God or be hidden from Him. The Psalmist writes that I was not invisible to Him in darkness because to Him it is like light. He sees my innermost being and knit me together in my mother's womb. In Him I am fearfully and wonderfully made.

The darkness that I experienced did not last forever, and even during the dark times I knew God was present, and step by step the darkness turned to light.

It began with an unhappy home life with a man, Bob W., my stepfather, who had a very hard life. He was born the same year as Bob Armstrong, shortly before the Depression. They were poor, and with his siblings, he ate watery soup. He remembered all his life how hungry he was.

Later in life, food would be clung to for comfort. His father had left the home and his mother Olive struggled to raise three children who were very close in age. They were not well-supervised and were allowed to play near the river while very young and not able to swim. God was merciful and saw in His providence that no matter what Bob would do with his life, God's good will prevailed.

Olive met Hank, who became a father figure to him. The family soon had enough to eat. Hank poached fish and game, and starvation was staved off by selling some of the catch.

Despite these odds, Bob W. grew into a big kid with a powerful body. His stepfather, who was a huge man, and mother would rent Bob W. to farmers, who would pay his mother and Hank his wages.

After graduation from high school, he went into the Air Force and became a skilled machinist, rising steadily in rank demonstrating a high level of skill and confidence to those above him. He was able to eat three meals a day, made a good wage, and for the first time led an independent life. Had he stayed, his life may have been better.

However, he chose to leave the Air Force. Upon his return he discovered that his parents had sold or given his things away. He did the work he knew, such as felling timber and driving trucks. While he was good at both, he never attempted to manage or own his own business. Though he had tasted success, he was fearful of losing what he had and would always say even when he was younger it was too late to now. This became the refrain of his life.

It is said that unhealthy people attract other unhealthy people, and he married someone who was more troubled than he was. It was a marriage that was violent and abusive and ended in divorce in 1963.

Upon the marriage of my mother to Bob W. in 1965, he gained a measure of stability with clearly defined boundaries that did not exist with his previous marriage. There was no drinking, he was put on a budget, debts were paid, and there would be no direct physical violence.

Wedding 1965 *New Family 1966-1967*

In 1966 my sister was born, and there were two first-born children. I was relegated to a secondary position.

My biological father was Italian, and Bob W. was German or Dutch. He and my sister had blondish hair with beautiful blue eyes. My heritage is Irish and Italian, so I had darker skin, black hair, and brown eyes. I was the strange bird in the family nest, and I was treated as such by him.

His method of parenting in my case was a grudging acceptance that I was there as well as a palpable dismissiveness. He could also be cruel; an example of this was one Christmas he decided to use the strange bird in his nest for target practice.

While sitting in his chair, he used a slingshot to shoot cigarette butts at me from across the room while I was drawing. I still remember his laughter and feeling the fear and humiliation while ducking to avoid the nasty missiles.

This memory foreshadowed my life. I began to avoid situations that I perceived could harm me and externally and internally duck for cover by avoiding the risk of being too close to people. I lived in an emotional defensive crouch, with fear and anxiety rather than faith and love.

In 1969, his twelve-year-old, truly lovely and vivacious daughter, Bobette, passed away, which nearly destroyed him. From 1969 until his repose, we were not allowed to mention her name. My mom worked at a small store in the '70s called K and K Food Ranch and was held up at gunpoint. She was the only one I trusted; I knew that if she died my future was uncertain. When she worked nights, I would stay awake until I heard the car arrive.

I learned to survive like a feral cat by observing my surroundings and keeping my council. I watched how he treated his stepdaughter Cindy who was his former wife's daughter and knew that she and I were not different in where we stood, within the family. Unfortunately, this created a suspicion of others' motives that kept me safe but aloof from others.

She had not been adopted by him and had no legal standing. I knew at some level that this was not what I wanted. In 1974, during a thaw in the fear after a trip to Disneyland, I asked to be adopted.

Trip to Disneyland 1974

This changed my status in the family but not necessarily the treatment. I had the security of being a legal son and that I could not be shunted away or forgotten if my mom died. However, my relationship with my stepfather remained cold and distant.

His abusive childhood with its neglectful parenting gave him a limited context on how to be a successful adult or parent. He feared life and risk and had little knowledge on how to have a meaningful life nor how to raise children.

He was not capable of being light to children. Rather, like a black hole, his deep need for attention and fears meant that all light and attention be focused on him, and he resented it when it shone on others.

He also emulated his parents in the way he treated his children. He enjoyed giving us jobs to do such as chopping and stacking wood, mowing the lawn, etc. The work was not hard work but the heart behind it was. There was no let's do it together and enjoy each other's company. We were there to do the tasks while he watched TV.

I looked at everything through the prisms of security and survival and there were three things I trusted: God, my mother, and books. God was always present. I perceived Him in the woods and mountains of Washington and in going to church with my grandmother. My mother who provided stability was counterweight for me with Bob

W., and books offered the possibilities of different realities. Through them I learned that there were different worlds and options that could be chosen. This gave me hope and the will to not quit.

I lived life looking out from a confined and very small internal box and was not well socialized. As a child I was considered immature and a brat, and I was. I ate too much to compensate for the stress and was fat. I took Tums because I was anxious, I was loud because I was not heard, I was mean to others because I did not know how to interact.

I acted out because I did not know how to get attention properly. In elementary school, I was clueless and slow, my desk pushed to the front. I did not read until third grade because I could not see the board and needed glasses, but the optometrist thought otherwise.

Childhood and young adulthood were made bearable by the friends who God gave me along the way. God bless the teachers, peers, the pastors, and the priests who in their kindness encouraged and provided friendship along the way.

In middle school I kept away from the bigger kids, preferring quiet spaces like the library. I was more prepared to watch life from a distance than engage in it.

By high school, I was emotionally immature, living in an inner box of fear and anxiety that stunted my growth formed by reaction to circumstance rather than choosing and acting on the circumstances. As I grew older, I grew more determined and did not quit. I think at some level he appreciated it. He was concerned when I joined the Army and surprised that I made it, as was I.

My parents said if I wanted to go to college, I would have to pay for it. I had no idea how to do this and no knowledge how to apply for loans, grants, and considered myself not smart enough for scholarships.

The Army's Veterans Education Program was the solution. If one served three years, they would pay for four years of college. I made it through Basic Training, which gave a boost to my self-esteem and confidence and found that I could be successful.

Boot Camp at Fort Dix NJ in February. I have never experienced anything like either the cold or Boot Camp. By the grace of God, I made it through both.

Comments on the back of Photo

One of the most amusing calls me a tough little soldier. The truth was, I was more tenacious than tough. It was a way to go to college, and I was going to make sure that I did not fail.

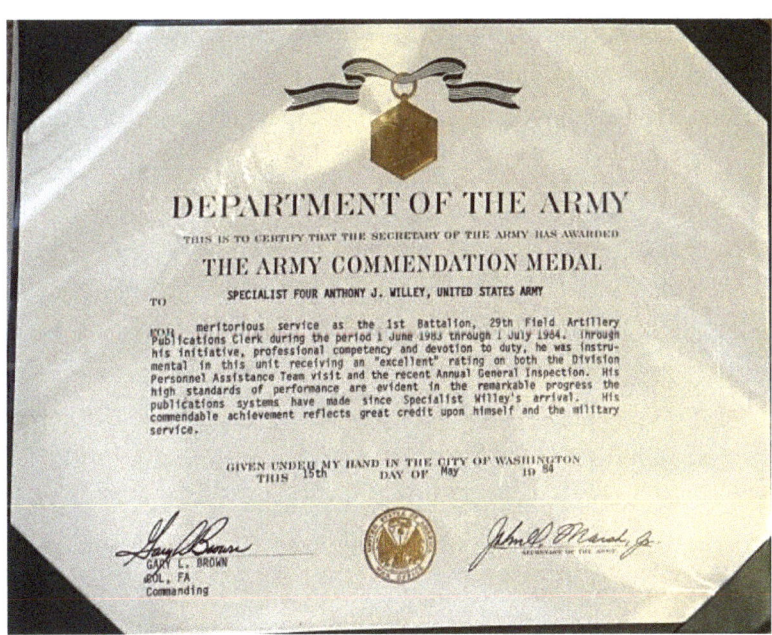

In 1984 I earned the Army Commendation Medal. I had never achieved any type of award before this, and it gave me a boost in confidence.

Like him, I left the military with the difference that I went back to school and earned a BA in behavioral science to help figure myself out. However, it was not a marketable degree, and like him I worked at low-paying jobs.

Again like him I needed the affirmation of others and was jealous when the light was not on me. Later Bob and Mary showed with their daily life that by walking toward Christ, I have Christ's light in me to be who I am meant to be. Living that light and love of others, I would not need to be the center of attention.

I was never truly at ease, secure, or confident in any social setting with peers. I knew something was wrong, but like Bob W., I did not have a clue how to change it.

He and his family had a strong aversion to religion of any sort. I vaguely remember his mother telling me that someone in her family who was religious committed a serious crime.

He did make a religious commitment in a church before dying. Like the thief on cross before Christ he asked in his simple way to be remembered in His Kingdom. I believe he was, and it was not too late.

He read Shakespeare in high school and could quote it and was a natural storyteller. If a TV show was missed, he could retell it as well as embellish it. As a former machinist he had a wonderful inventive mind and designed inventions like a grave digger.

He could be funny and caring, yet stunningly cruel and tone deaf to the feelings of others. As I matured and he grew older and sick, I felt sorry for this man who could not find his way out of his own inner box and into a happy life.

Bob W. had heart disease. He had a series of silent heart attacks and was medically retired while in his hospital bed in 1990. He lived for two years in declining health. I was living at another location when my mother called me and told me to come home because he was going to die. I had no idea how she knew, but I came back to the house. My sister and her son, who was a year old, was there, and we sat in the kitchen while he sat in his chair.

I went out to greet him but stopped. My nephew was sitting on his lap, and they both were covered in light. I had seen this light in an older patient at a hospital and learned that he had died the same day. Later I learned that this may have been the leaving of the soul from the body, and that we are creatures of light.

My nephew got off his lap and played. My mom glanced out and saw Bob W. in convulsions. My sister, who was heavily pregnant with her second son, and I lifted him off the chair and did CPR.

I did breaths, and she did chest percussions. I think we both knew it was futile, but we had to try. The firemen took over and told my mom they were impressed with the effort and that there was a heart rhythm, but it was the dying heart's last movements before stopping. We suspect that he passed at home and that they declared him dead at the hospital. The last time I saw him was in death. He was still, his mouth slightly open. I wept.

The legacy he left was a paradoxical puzzle consisting of pieces both light and dark which could not abide together. His personality could not become whole, and those divergent pieces tore him up inside as well as wounding others in the process. Yet he left lights in the persons of my sister and her three children, whom I love.

The hate of his cruelty, the loathing at his abuse, the love that was there in moments amid it. Finally, forgiveness was the only thing that stopped the battle of dark and light from tearing me up.

I carried this legacy for thirty years—the wounds from the dark pieces of his legacy and my responses to them—and looked for a path out.

A Dead-End Job Opens a Door of Opportunity

After Bob W.'s death, I had a long dry spell of low-paying jobs. I always said to myself when Bob W. thought I could not do anything, "I'll show you." Now I had no one to show.

The one that stands out the most was when I took care of clients with physical and developmental issues who were once institutionalized.

It was a tough job that involved dressing, feeding, and toileting adults. Their institutionalized behaviors reflected how they were treated by their caregivers, which was often abusive.

Working there was difficult because often these behaviors were the only way they knew how to interact with those who served them. It was a bruising experience. In addition, it did not pay a livable wage or offer insurance, and though I tried several things to become independent and make a livable wage, it was to no avail.

As difficult as it was, there were moments of grace. Two moments come to mind. The first was that I met a young man named Bum. Bum, at the time, was on staff with InterVarsity Christian Fellowship and was everything that I wanted to be. He was confident, strong, kind, and lived his faith.

He knew who he was and to whom he belonged. He had a solid inner core that radiated mental health, strength, and light. This gave him the freedom to not be distracted by insecurities and live fully. My inner core was soft clay in need of molding into a man of God.

Bob was the man who would mold my inner core that would become strong over time and who, like Bum, would know who he is and who he belonged to.

Another key moment was when a staff member at Service Alternatives noticed me talking to a child. She said that I would be a great teacher. It was a suggestion that would be the first of many steps toward independence and a way out from a being shy, scared, thirty-something man to one who was confident in God's love and grace.

In 1995 I took another risk and pursued the path out of poverty and dependence. I got a $20,000 loan and began a year-long course of study for a Masters in Teaching at City University. Like the Army, it was challenging, and I learned that I was capable of more than I believed. It was during this time that I began to explore the Orthodox faith.

Seeking the Warmth of Faith

I had been raised Roman Catholic and was religious as a kid. Most of my peers did sex, drugs, and rock and roll, while I did religion and explored churches.

My abstinence from these activities was not due to virtue but from fear and a total sense of inadequacy in relating to peers. I was sorry to not have known them but grateful that I did not participate in these activities. Looking back at where I was in my life, those activities would have turned an already fragile person into a mental disaster.

The search for God began in the Roman Catholic Church with my grandmother. It was there I first glimpsed the love of God in the Eucharist. Together we would walk to Immaculate Conception Church and attend the 5:00 p.m. Mass.

My beloved grandparent Joe and Agnes Morris. Joe was my grandmother's second husband. He passed in 1966.

My grandmother and I when I was in high school.

I felt a warmth in my heart and wanted more. Unfortunately, the changes that occurred in the Roman Catholic Church made finding that warmth elusive, if not impossible. I would only find it in the Orthodox Church.

Vatican II completely changed the Roman Catholic Church. The church from the nineteenth century to the early 1960s was one of tangible piety. Eucharistic Visitation, where one would contemplate the presence of Christ, were no longer in vogue by the 1970s.

The altars were turned westward, the old tabernacles that were majestic because they contained the reserve sacrament were replaced with ugly boxes covered with the fad art of the 1960s. Fasting was eliminated, the stations of the cross neglected, the classical music replaced with guitar masses. The form of the Mass was replaced with a modern version that was short both in length and in spiritual content. Tangibles that generations of Catholics hung onto were no more.

These absences left a longing for the presence of Christ, and trying to find that "warmth of faith," I explored the Episcopal and Pentecostal churches and other faith groups.

From 1987 to 1990, I attended Northwest Assembly of God Bible School. What stuck with me was that if you were not born into the Assemblies of God and were from the Roman Catholic faith, you did not really belong.

It was ironic because it was the same perception I had about the Orthodox Church. The Assemblies of God were right. I did not belong because I was culturally Catholic and liturgically oriented and did not fit.

Thankfully my perception was wrong about the Orthodox Church. Later my friend Doug, who is an Assembly of God Minister and who was my mentor and pastor while I attended Northwest College, understood this dilemma and thought the Orthodox Church was a good choice for me.

Christopher

An event occurred twenty-seven years earlier that would change the lives of Bob and Mary and those who would meet them in the future.

Mary Armstrong Scrapbook courtesy of John Goddard

Jesus said, "Let the little children come to me, and do not hinder them, for the Kingdom of Heaven belongs to such as these" (Matthew 19:14).

The beginning of Bob and Mary's life together and the people they would touch begins with the brief life of Jack and Mary's second son, Christopher.

Christopher's early death was the pivot point in the lives of Bob and Mary. In 1962, when Chris was born, Jack and Mary's marriage was apparently healthy. By 1967, it was over due to Jack's alcoholism. Mary was a single mother of three children.

Bob was divorced and both were attending the same church. Bob was superintendent of the Sunday school and Mary a teacher.

Chris grew into a remarkable little boy for his age with depth and athletic ability that were beyond the expectations of a five-year-old. Mary and her boys were visiting her father at his Arizona home.

At twilight, Chris was sitting quietly with his back against the stucco wall of his grandfather's house.

His grandfather asked, "What are you looking at, Chris?"

He replied, "I'm just listening to the night." The child was just five and very deep. The potential of this boy who could throw a football and think deeply was truly great and found its perfection in Heaven (Armstrong, 106-107).

Another time while Mary was visiting her father, they noticed that Christopher was lagging behind the other kids at the beach. This was unusual for a child of this age, especially for Christopher, who gave his all to keep up.

Mary asked her father, who was a pediatrician, to look at Christopher and find out what was wrong with him. Dr. Vaughn looked down his grandson's throat, and to his horror, found a tumor. He told Mary that she needed to get him to a doctor immediately for further tests, which she did.

Christopher was diagnosed with leukemia in April 1968. The diagnosis for leukemia in 1968 was usually terminal. There were not many treatment options with chemotherapy, which was the only real option. However, this was for adults, not for a five-year-old.

This treatment was beyond painful for both Christopher physically and Mary as the mother of a very ill child. Bob, observant and compassionate, saw what was happening and gave her his business card, which said, Robert Armstrong, USC Director of Personnel, with his personal number.

One day Chris's temperature reached 105.5, and he was throwing up blood. There was no one available to help her. Mary's father was visiting her sister in Massachusetts; Dr. Goddard, Chris's father, was in Russia at a medical convention; and Mary's brother was serving in Vietnam. Mary called Bob at midnight. "I am so sorry to bother you, but I need some help here."

True to his word, he was there for her.

She bundled Christopher in the backseat of the car, walked up the hill, and met Bob in the lobby. He then sat with Christopher while she checked him in. An hour later they both donated platelets for Chris.

All three of them were walking up a hill toward the Kingdom of God. Desperately sick Chris was on his way home into the arms of the Savior. Mary was walking like the mother of Christ, knowing that her son would likely not make it. Bob was doing for the least of his brethren by supporting Mary, attending to Chris, and donating his blood for him.

His continued to support Mary and Chris by providing transportation for the mother and son as well as transfusions for Chris. They walked together, supporting Chris, until Chris was safely in the arms of Christ.

Marriage

Chris reposed six weeks from the initial diagnosis.

To quote the beautifully written obituary, "Through the crucible of Chris's death, Robert and Mary fell headlong in love and married November 9, 1968." (*Everett Herald*, November 25 to 26, 2015.)

It was on this date unknown to them then that Christ would reach thousands of lives through them.

Pictures courtesy John Goddard

Bob said years later on his deathbed that "Love trumps all." Love of God, love for each other, and love for Christopher trumped the tragedy of Christopher's death. He is now reunited with his mother and the man who followed Christ in giving his blood for him.

Pictures courtesy John Goddard

Bob's Life: A Sketch

DIVORCE IN BOB'S FAMILY

Bob's family had a history of divorce. It began with his grandmother.

His grandmother's marriage had ended, and his mother was raised by her mother. Her mother trained her how to survive in life with sewing but not how to live a life in faith and love.

BOB'S PARENTS

Robert Henry Armstrong was born July 24, 1928, to Robert and Penny Armstrong in Phoenix, Arizona. His father was a lawyer, and mother a seamstress.

His father left the marriage when Bob was nine, and he never understood why. Bob always wondered why and never found an answer. Adding to this pain, Bob had very little contact with him in the intervening years.

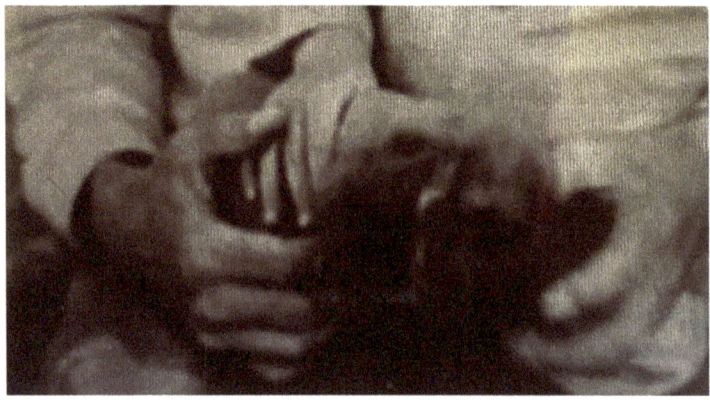

Enlargement of Bob with Dad 1931

This is an enlargement of the picture of Bob, his pup, and his dad. This is a picture of a son content in the arms of his father. Notice how his dad is holding the pup and touching Bob's hand. Notice that both are safe, secure, content.

Then imagine that Bob's parents' marriage ends. That the father does not visit or come back. This picture is a symbol of every child's happiness with his father, but in Bob's case it was a symbol of loss that he never got over or understood.

What he did, which will be shown later, is that he loved God, his wife, and children and reached out and touched many by being a mentor and a godfather to all who had the joy of loving him. He used this cross to love God and others as himself.

AFTER BOB'S FATHER LEFT

His mother was a superb seamstress, and her hard work ensured Bob had the opportunity to have a high-quality childhood and the internal means to be a success. Bob recalled much later in life that his mother would sit through double features of cowboy movies with him. **Caregiving for Your Loved Ones, p.198**

This is documented in six precious letters between Bob and Jacob McGinnis for a Generations Project that Jacob did for school. It is a precious cache and gives Bob an opportunity to tell his story.

> Hi Jacob,
>
> I'm looking forward to being your correspondent for your class project. Thank you for asking Mary & me to fill this role for you. Yes, we will include notes from my childhood.
>
> I was born on July 24, 1928 in Phoenix Arizona, before air conditioning and 69 years before your birth. I had several dogs: my favorite was a springer spaniel named Bird, who was black and white. Unfortunately he bit a boy who was teasing him, so my family had to find another home for him. I also remember a cocker spaniel named Chee Chee, plus a rabbit I received at Easter, who promptly escaped through the hedge into our neighbors' yard and was never seen again. I even raised twenty-five chickens and two turkeys, until the city of Phoenix said we had to get rid of them after they changed the zoning rules.
>
> Sunday afternoons involved, quite often, dinner with my grandfather and grandmother. They had a German shepherd named Bruno, whom I loved to play with. I had several buds, both boys and girls, and we used to get together at each other's homes for play ad lunch. The O'Malleys lived next door, and Ted and Ann were close-by playmates. Their Dad would occasionally bring home rented 16mm movies which he would run on his projector. Much fun. Their Dad also had a hobby of model railroads, and it was fun to watch him run his trains.
>
> My grammar school was grades K-8, then on to high school, grades 9 - 12. I enjoyed school. The emphasis was more on basics, the 3-R's, without a lot of supplemental subjects, although I can remember music, art, and a wood shop class for two years where I made a desk and a small box. We had to pass a test on the Constitution and history of both the United States and Arizona to graduate from both schools. You have more homework than I had. I don't know which era had the hardest school.
>
> We did not have school buses because we were in the city. I rode to school with my father on his way to work until I receive a bicycle, and I could ride that to my grade, grammar, and high schools. In the winter it could be both cold and even rainy. Recess was a lot of fun with one period of physical education where we played pickup, football, or softball games. Girls played jump rope and hopscotch. In grammar school we brought our lunch - P.B. & J. with rabbit food. In high school there was a cafeteria, although I generally brought my own lunch - baloney sandwiches as well as P.B. & J.
>
> I played the accordion and also the piano, but do not have any musical talent, sadly.
>
> History was my favorite subject and the sciences, physics ad chemistry, were my least favorites. I did enjoy biology and Latin. In high school I was in R.O.T.C. (military marching and drill) for four years.
>
> Christmas and Thanksgiving were spent with close family friends - always a lot of fun. My most memorable present was a single-shot .22 caliber rifle with 500 rounds of ammunition. I taught our children gun safety with that gun. We all enjoyed plinking and shooting at tin cans.

For Halloween I would quite often dress up like a hobo and darken my face with a blackened cork. I had a bandana with candy inside tied around a stick and carried over my shoulder.

I can't remember my first present, but I did receive a number of books from family friends which I always enjoyed.

Vacations in the summers were generally spent at a family cabin in the mountains, 6000 feet elevation, where it was cool and there were rocks and mountains to climb, plus birthday parties and taffy pulls and games. On Saturdays, a trip to the grocery store seven miles away was fun. I got to spend time at the library while my mother shopped. As a teenager, sometimes a parent would drive a bunch of us into town, Prescott, for a movie.

Summer time was time off from church When we were in Phoenix I went to Sunday School, which I really enjoyed. Church was about an hour as I recall. Sunday afternoon, as time passed, was spent doing homework and getting ready for school on Monday, The radio was big source of entertainment, and listening to "Amos and Andy" was fun.

I hope this gets us started on early childhood, and even into my teens I am looking forward to your next letter. Please let me know if you need clarification or have questions.

Your Godfather and friend,

Bob

Letter courtesy Jacob McGinnis

Pictures courtesy John Goddard

YOUTH AND ROUTINE

This letter combined with the pictures shows a strong supportive family. There was a weekly rhythm to life, Sunday dinners with his grandparents, a rigorous curriculum in school, along with a social life spent with friends.

Bob's mother supported and encouraged him in his growth from boy to young man. He did not let the pain of the absence of his father stop him from living life to the fullest.

Looking at the pictures, one sees someone who enjoyed the outdoors as well as the structure and adventure of scouts and ROTC.

HOLIDAY STRUCTURE

Halloween

Bob would dress up as a hobo with a satchel of candy carried on a stick. I was in an antique store and found this hobo mouse. It reminded me of what Bob's costume might have looked like.

Thanksgiving and Christmas

He writes that Thanksgiving and Christmas were spent with family and close friends and that a memorable gift was single-shot .22 rifle with 500 rounds. Bob and his friends enjoyed shooting tin cans. Later he would teach his children gun safety with that same gun.

The seeds for Bob's interest in Sunday school is on the second page of the letter where he mentions he really enjoyed this. Later in life he would meet Mary at church where she was a Sunday school teacher and he the superintendent. The future was planted in his youth and would bloom and bear fruit as an adult.

Summers In Iron Springs
Summers were spent at the family cabin at Iron Springs. With an elevation of 6,000 feet, it was an ideal for relief from the intense heat of the summer sun.

Here he would climb rocks with friends and go to taffy pulls and birthday parties.

Going shopping was a fun occasion in nearby Prescott, and while his mother shopped, he would spend time in the library as teenagers. A parent would sometimes take them to a movie in Prescott.

Sundays
Sunday was spent at church and getting ready for the following week by doing homework.

SOCIAL LIFE
In letter two we catch a glimpse of Bob's social life. He was popular, enjoyed birthday parties, movies, dates, and dances with friends from his childhood. This required that he worked.

Work
Bob started to work when he was sixteen in Phoenix. Those jobs included working in a metal shop, tire dealer, vegetable packing shop and a trailer dealer. Bob writes a line that foreshadowed his whole life. **"I was a helper, doing odd jobs such as clean up and helping where needed."** He was there when needed, especially for Mary and Christopher in 1968. **Letter 2**

This routine helped create the inner core of Bob that set him up for success in attending and graduating from Stanford. It also gave him the resiliency to survive and thrive with future challenges.

Bob enjoyed dancing the foxtrot and waltzes, and he also enjoyed an active social life.

Upon graduation he was employed by Sears in merchandising. He took "additional college courses in psychology, management, wage and salary and other areas." He would later head the Personnel Department at USC and other schools. People were always his love, interest, and forte.

Bob would wed his first wife, Nancy, and have two children. The marriage would sadly end in the 1960s, and in 1968 he would wed Mary.

Scrapbook pages courtesy of John Goddard
Bob and Nancy's daughters

Two informal pictures of Bob with his daughters during their time at Lake Arrowhead. The photo on the left is a birthday, and the photo on the right shows Bob's sense of humor.

Scrapbook pages created by Mary Armstrong courtesy of John Goddard

A Sketch of Mary's Life

Mary had deep roots in California. She was born March 12, 1934, in Santa Monica, California, to John and Helen Vaughn.

Santa Monica in the thirties and forties was idyllic. Mary and Margaret would walk to nearby Rustic Canyon. A block-long Cecil Brunner Rose Bush would be there to greet them with its scent before they would see it. On Mother's Day the sisters would prepare nosegays for their mother and set it at their mother's place at the table.

Source: Mary Armstrong Scrapbook: Growing up in Santa Monica

Scrapbook pages courtesy of John Goddard

Mary and Margaret explored the paradise of their childhood home. As the breezes of the ocean, eucalyptus, and honey suckles surrounded them they made forts from the pine needles, climbed trees, caught polliwogs, picked Miners Lettuce, and romped with their dogs. **Source: Mary Armstrong Scrapbook: Growing up in Santa Monica. Courtesy John Goddard**

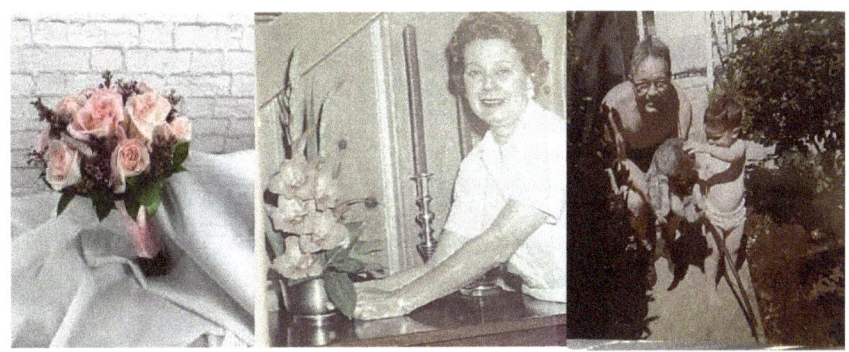

A nosegay
Photos courtesy of John Goddard

Scrapbook pages courtesy of John Goddard

I asked John what made Mary the way she was. He said Mary was born of two very dynamic and educated people. Dr. John Vaughn and Helen were both graduates of Stanford University.

Dr. and Mrs. Vaughn gave their children the tools they would need to be successful.

The first lesson was good manners. They were respectful of their parents. They did not repeat adult conversation and learned to answer the phone politely and take accurate messages.

The second was that they received an excellent education at home through purposeful conversation at the dinner table. They were to come prepared to share a topic. Both would be required to memorize and recite Christ's Sermon on Mount as well as Shakespeare's Polonius's Advice to Laertes.

Polonius's Advice to Laertes
Hamlet I, iii, 55-81

LORD POLONIUS
Yet here, Laertes! aboard, aboard, for shame!
The wind sits in the shoulder of your sail,
And you are stay'd for. There; my blessing with thee!
And these few precepts in thy memory
See thou character. Give thy thoughts no tongue,
Nor any unproportioned thought his act.
Be thou familiar, but by no means vulgar.
Those friends thou hast, and their adoption tried,
Grapple them to thy soul with hoops of steel;
But do not dull thy palm with entertainment
Of each new-hatch'd, unfledged comrade. Beware
Of entrance to a quarrel, but being in,
Bear't that the opposed may beware of thee.
Give every man thy ear, but few thy voice;
Take each man's censure, but reserve thy judgment.
Costly thy habit as thy purse can buy,
But not express'd in fancy; rich, not gaudy;
For the apparel oft proclaims the man,
And they in France of the best rank and station
Are of a most select and generous chief in that.
Neither a borrower nor a lender be;
For loan oft loses both itself and friend,
And borrowing dulls the edge of husbandry.
This above all: to thine own self be true,
And it must follow, as the night the day,
Thou canst not then be false to any man.
Farewell: my blessing season this in thee!

In assigning these two readings, Mary's parents laid a spiritual and moral foundation that Mary was to build upon for the rest of her life. **Mary Armstrong Scrapbook: Growing up in Santa Monica**

Another seed was growing as well. As a young child, she walked into the Catholic church and sat and enjoyed "the blue candles and the statue of Christ above the altar." As she grew, she continued to visit the church.
Our Hearts' True Home p. 168

Across from Rustic Creek was the Canyon School that both attended. In the Spring they would study the indigenous plants of the area. They became field scientists and learned to not only observe the beauty of plants but their function. This was natural coming from a father who was a doctor and mother who was a nurse.
Source: Mary Armstrong Scrapbook: Growing up in Santa Monica

A second seed was planted in the family's place of worship at Santa Monica Presbyterian Church by a first-grade Sunday school teacher named Miss Bacon who said, **"If we listen, we can hear God's voice."** Mary never forgot this and she would listen to God the rest of her life. **Source: Mary Armstrong Scrapbook: Growing up in Santa Monica**

> Gardening has been a beloved hobby of many generations of Vaughns. On the balmy afternoon of December 7, 1941, Grandfather John troweled mortar between slabs of rose hued flagstone, Grandma Helen pruned flowers in bright ceramic pots, while Mom and Aunt Mimi played on the swing set. As always, the family's large brown Zenith radio was on. Suddenly a man's somber voice broke in, to announce that Pearl Harbor, Hawaii, was being bombed by Japanese planes. Our peaceful afternoon abruptly ended as we rushed to the radio, listening in disbelief. We did not know it then, but at that moment everything in our lives was to change forever.

Scrapbook picture courtesy John Goddard

This idyllic life was interrupted with World War II.

Dr. and Mrs. Vaughn were in the medical field and steeped in the sciences that support them. There is a plan and order for everything a doctor and nurse do. John used the example of giving a patient a medication. You don't just pull it out of the bottle and pop it in their mouth. You make sure the right medication is given by using a checklist.

Do I have the right medication for the patient? Does the dosage meet the needs of the patient? Has there been a change to the medication according to the chart? How is the medication to be delivered? After those questions are answered then the medication can be given.

Helen kept her career and family going with this paradigm in mind while her husband served in World War II. Alone with three children she moved from Santa Monica to Conneaut, Ohio, to live with Helen's mother while Dr. Vaughn was serving in the South Pacific during World War II.

Mary internalized her mother Helen's organizational skills and practiced them throughout her life in school, in her careers, as nurse, author, and homemaker.

In their life together Bob's need for routine complimented Mary's organizational skills and served both well. These skills would be needed in their five moves from 1970 to 1990.

Another memory learned from her mother was to create beauty in her home, no matter where they were or how simple the material. She also got her keen sense of humor from her as well as how her mother's Scotch Irish heritage had sprinkled her days with joy, like the morning she climbed down a ladder and lowered one leg-shoe, sock, and all-into a pail of sudsy water. Mary continues, "I waited, not sure how to respond, until she burst out into peals of laughter."

Helen's mastery of relocating a household and running it independently, as well as creating beauty and her parent's gifts for connecting with others, was also emulated by their daughter.

Having a love for words, she wanted to be a writer, but her father said that there were many starving writers out there and it would be better to have a career so that you could put food on the table. Mary took this advice with the goal of becoming a nurse.

Well-prepared by her parents and primed for success, she was admitted to Stanford in 1952. **Interview with John**

STANFORD

The years at Stanford were an engaging challenge for Mary. Stanford then was not the maelstrom of politics it is today; rather, it was a place of academic excellence and learning with high standards and a rigorous curriculum.

It was the place to go for a superb education and a degree that had weight and value worldwide. Mary's drive, curiosity, and her goal-oriented personality made Stanford a place of deep satisfaction and achievement for her. The first two years were spent on undergraduate requirements before transferring to the School of Nursing.
Mary Armstrong Stanford University Page

Included in the Scrapbook page is the story of Mr. Buttons. It is the only story I recall Mary telling, and reading the account on the scrapbook page, it was tougher than she let on. First it was fifteen hours a week and Mary and cohort had to know all the muscles, veins, organs, vascular systems. Second it was with a human body, not a cat, dog, or pig. This was real education and science. **Mary Armstrong Stanford University Page**

Mary recalled that she studied for hours for the final test with the cadaver and that the doctor came in, pointed to a specific part of the cadaver, and asked her to identify it. She answered correctly and that was it. She seemed both relieved and disappointed, and knowing Mary I can understand why.
Mary Armstrong Stanford University Page

Mary Armstrong Stanford University Page
Courtesy, John Goddard

What drew me in was the name and the mystery of why there was a button where his navel was. However, what I remember most from the conversation was the deep reverence and respect that all had for the cadaver. It was once a person and deserved to be treated with respect. **Mary Armstrong Stanford University Page**

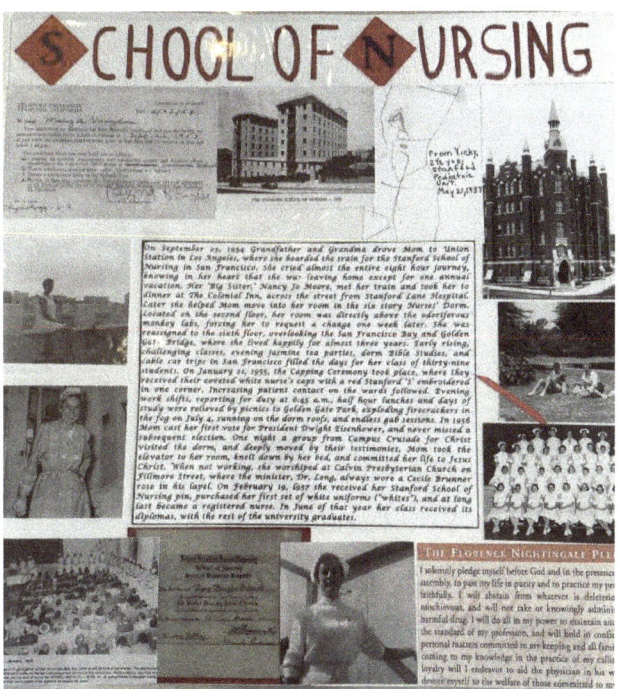

Mary Armstrong Stanford School of Nursing page
Courtesy, John Goddard

On September 23, 1954, Mary was on her way to Stanford School of Nursing in San Francisco. Her father drove her to Union Train Station in Los Angeles to San Francisco. Although Mary had been away from home and going to university, she was still close to home and within easy reach of family, and there was only one vacation period. She wept all the way there and was met by Nancy Jo Moore, her "Big Sister" who would help her navigate the new world of Stanford Nursing. Nancy Jo was a lifelong friend to Mary and a lovely kind lady. **Mary Armstrong School of Nursing Scrapbook**

The program was three years and except for a brief time she lived on the sixth floor with a view of San Francisco Bay and the Golden Gate Bridge; it was likely the setting and inspiration for her book, *Golden Gate Morning*, which Mary would write decades later. **Mary Armstrong School of Nursing Scrapbook**

Once Mary arrived, her drive and curiosity kicked in and she pursued her life and studies with gusto. There were the fun times, like evening jasmine tea parties and cable car rides, but after the capping ceremony on January 25, 1955, where she received her nurse's cap with the red Stanford S embroidered in one corner, she became very busy. **Mary Armstrong School of Nursing Scrapbook**

The academic merged into the practical with patient contact in the morning, short half-hour lunches, and ward time in the evening. This was tailor-made for Mary; it was an opportunity to plan and hone her medical nursing skills. **Mary Armstrong School of Nursing Scrapbook**

She was also to learn from her first-grade Sunday school teacher, Miss Bacon, who said, **"If we listen, we can hear God's voice." Source: Mary Armstrong Scrapbook: Growing up in Santa Monica**

Mary heard God's voice in a group from Campus Crusade who shared their stories of Christ's love; going to her room she knelt and committed her life to Jesus Christ.

She wrote in her account of her faith journey, "I had invited Jesus Christ into my life when I was twenty years old. I didn't know much about the Bible then, but I surrendered my heart to Jesus in response to the unconditional love He showed through his death on the cross. After an evening in Bible Study in my nursing school dorm, I knelt by my bed on the sixth floor and turned my life over to Jesus." **Our Heart True Home, p. 167.**

When not working she attended Calvary Presbyterian Church, pastored by Dr. Long, who always wore a Cecille Brunner rose in his lapel. Mary heard God's voice and followed it where it led her. **Mary Armstrong School of Nursing Scrapbook**

On March 9, 1957, Mary achieved her goal of becoming a registered nurse. The prized Stanford Nursing pin and her first Uniform were the tangible evidence of this achievement, and she graduated with her class the following June. Mary and Jack Goddard began their lives together the same year. **Mary Armstrong School of Nursing Scrapbook**

GOALS IN WRITING THUS FAR

My goals thus far were three-fold. First, I wanted to provide the background of my youth and how Bob and Mary were the answer to the way out of box I was in.

Second, I wanted to show the impact of Christopher's passing in the story. This is where the Bob and Mary that so many knew and loved began.

Third, I wanted to sketch their lives. Many like myself see older people as ordinary, and only in knowing and loving them do we get a hint that there is a lifetime of experience behind the facade of age.

I did not know them when they were young, and they covered themselves with a cloak of humility. Their present lives were more important to them than their past. Their values and faith, though, were ageless, and what mattered was living them in the present.

> How do you spell sports paradise? Lake Arrowhead and Palo Cedro, California! During the wonderful two years Leslie lived with us at the lake, she became a cheerleader in the ninth grade. Matt and I entered full bore into almost every sport available: I played baseball for the Pirates, was a member of the Rim High School ski team, ran cross country, water skied on every lake I could find, and loved to sail our 16' Hobie Cat and other sailboats, which earned me a position as a paid crew member for several summers. Matt played baseball for the Dodgers and Pirates, loved to water ski, played football throughout his school years, and greatly enjoyed deer hunting, bringing home a 4-point buck to Palo Cedro. Grandfather's legendary aluminum rowboat, "Pee Wee," and power boat, "Little Red," provided endless hours of exploration and water skiing, while trips to his house in the desert offered chances for target practice. The grief of searing loss also visited our family during those joyful years, including Grandfather's earthly departure on Thanksgiving weekend, 1972, and Dad's repose on October 15, 1975. May their memories be eternal!

A Sketch Lake Arrowhead
Courtesy, John Goddard

John's recollections of Lake Arrowhead.
Courtesy, John Goddard

Courtesy, John Goddard

It is important to reflect the impact of the Armstrong Goddard Family at Lake Arrowhead. Here can be seen Bob and Mary's brilliance in choosing a setting to bring up young men and the sacrifices that come with it.

Bob and Mary lived in a beautiful house at Lake Arrowhead, California, from 1970 to 1978. Bob was Director of Personnel at Riverside Community College and Mary a school nurse.

John recalls this time at Lake Arrowhead as bliss. Bob and Mary felt it would be a good move for their family. It was small-town California and a pleasant and healthy contrast to southern California with a beautiful lake for watercraft activities such as exploring the lake and water skiing.

In addition, it provided ample sporting opportunities for John and Matt who were of the age to need an outlet for their abundant energy.

This energy found outlets in cross-country skiing. John played baseball and was a member of the ski team, as well as ran cross-country, while Matt played baseball and football, waterskied, and hunted.

They would also go to their grandfather's house in the desert for target practice as Bob did as a boy and into adulthood.

Bob at nineteen target shooting. Teaching shooting in the 1970s to John and Matt.
Courtesy, John Goddard

They were trusted to know what to do with guns and to be responsible while using them in hunting or sport. Why is this important? John and his brother were given the gift to reach their full potential in their development as young men in mind and body.

They not only had an outlet for their energy and Bob's principled guidance but were given independence to try things such as going to the lake in a boat for the day. John learned he could earn money while using his expertise on sailboats as a paid crew.

Another outlet was work, and John recalls he and Bob cutting wood to heat the home. Those who have tried to cut wood know that it is not as easy as it looks.

The ax must hit at the right place for it to cut effectively. Bob knew how to cut through knots and could find the sweet spot on any piece. John learned through cutting a lot of wood and became excellent at it. Bob imparted some wisdom: "Chop your wood and it will warm you twice." The exercise and the fellowship of working together one is warmth once; the second is the burning for warmth.

The choice of this setting demonstrates the deep love and commitment that Bob and Mary had for their sons. Bob commuted an hour each way to Riverside to work leaving early in the morning from home and arriving back around six at night. They knew that giving their sons the opportunity to develop as young men was critical to their being successful adults. They realized that for young men to mature they needed to be encouraged, guided, mentored, and supported. They were right and because of their investment both became great men.

The Armstrongs were being prepared to be godparents to numerous adults and young people and they would need to employ everything they learned in the following years.

As idyllic as these years were, the family endured loss and pain. The first was before the move to Lake Arrowhead, Mary's dear mother Helen. Mother and daughter loved flowers and gardening. The gardens in each of Bob and Mary's homes were places she could go to reconnect with nature and Creator.

Mary learned of her mother's quiet courage in the six weeks between her diagnosis of cancer and her passing. She writes, "I discovered new dimensions of my mother's character, a quiet courage camouflaged by frequent laughter." She continues, "One bright morning I brought her a small bouquet of strawberry pink carnations. Beaming, she inhaled their cinnamon-sweet scent." Helen exclaimed, "I've always loved carnations! They smell like the garden on a hot summer day." **Quiet Moments for Parents and Other Caregivers, p. 90**

Two years later her beloved father would pass suddenly. John's father Dr. John Goddard would follow in 1975, but through all this with Bob and her family by her side and God over all of them they walked on with faith and love.

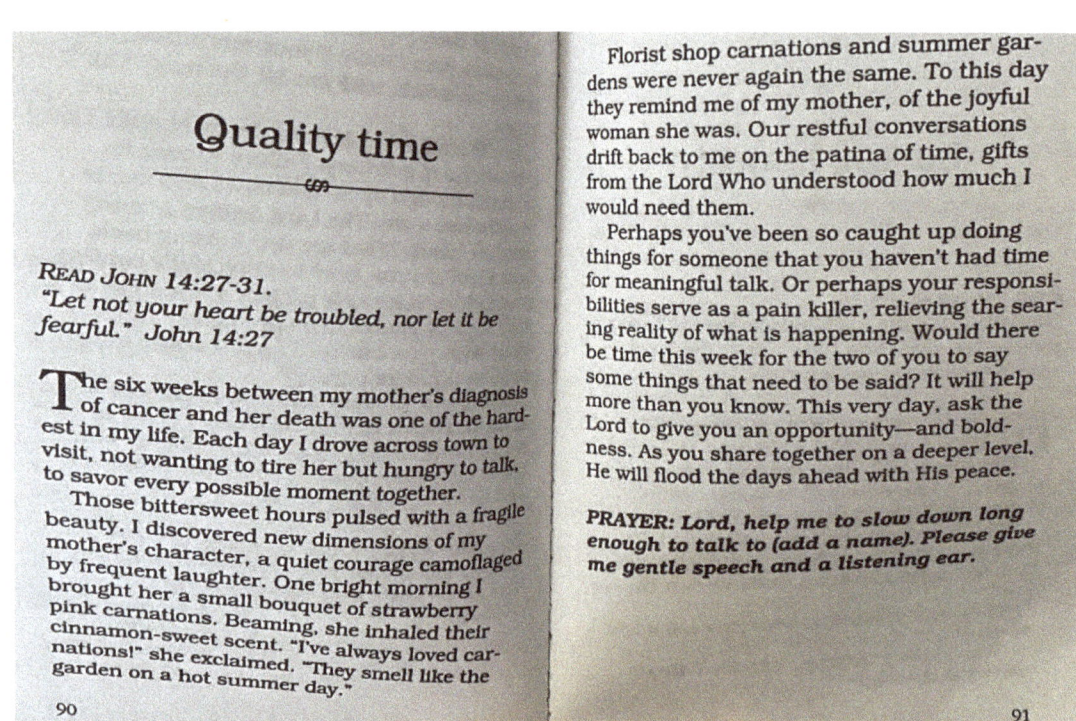

Quiet Moments for Parents and Other Caregivers, p. 90-91

RETIRED LIFE

Bob had retired at sixty-two from Whitworth College, and they slowly moved toward the Northwest. First to Spokane and as the family expanded and moved to the Northwest, they moved to Camano Island. Bob and Mary were very considerate and did not want to crowd their children but found that Camano Island was not close or convenient to where they lived. They then moved to Marysville, Washington, and lived there for twenty-six years.

The Writer

Dr. Vaughn's pragmatic advice to go to school and get an occupation to put food on the table sustained her and her sons through divorce as well as the illness and loss of Christopher when she was the sole breadwinner.

Now with both retired, Mary could write and share the lessons that she and Bob experienced as caregivers for his beloved mother. *Caregiving for Your Loved Ones* was published in 1990, followed by *Quiet Moments for Caregivers* and *Golden Gate Morning* in 1992. In addition, Mary edited several books and contributed to numerous articles and books. One of those books, *Our Hearts' True Home*, was edited by Virginia Nieuwsma.

In my opinion one of the most important of her works is *Caregiving for Your Loved Ones*. This book documents two years in the 1980s when the Armstrongs provided care to his aged mother Penny. Each event in life creates opportunities for the future if we have the courage to go through them.

Just as the trauma of Christopher's passing provided a catalyst for the marriage and union between Bob and Mary, the caregiving of Penny equipped them with the additional skills of caring for eighty godchildren and the numerous people who they encountered. The process was not easy as Mary recalls her caregiving experience in *Caregiving for Your Loved Ones*, 219.

CAREGIVING AND KEY LESSONS OF FAITH

Mary found "that the fruit of the Spirit doesn't ripen after all the jobs are done. The fruit grows in the midst of the work, probably because of it." Mary, who was always very organized, learned to accept this because, "Drudgery, interruptions, and confusion came from the outside . . . The Spirit works within, if only I give him a chance." Mary had always listened to God, and now she was listening to Him and seeing him act amidst the challenges of her life. Dr. Paul Lennox, an Oxford Professor emeritus of Mathematics, concurs with this when he says about the problems of life, "Solving those problems is living." In doing this she learned how to find her way to loving Penny with the cross as the bridge. **Why I believe in God, Dr. John Lennox, Interviewed by Dr. Amy Orr-Ewing. YouTube, 20 October 2023**

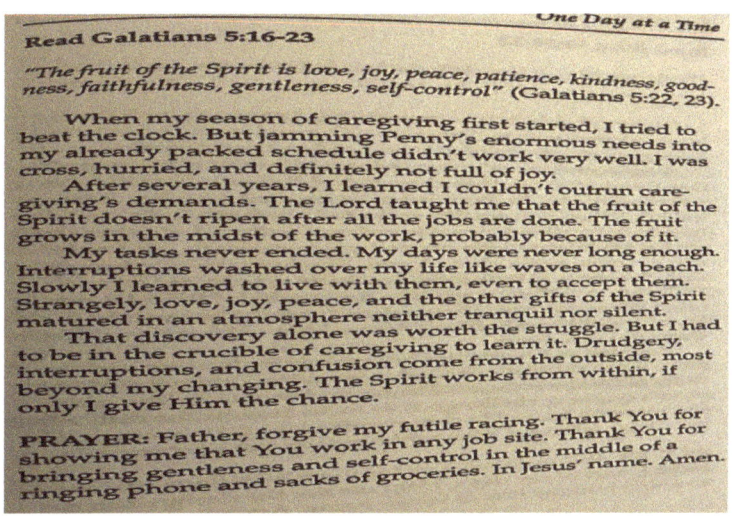

LEARNING TO LOVE THE DIFFICULT

For example, Mary recalls asking Penny how she liked her birthday party. Penny chose to not recall it. When Mary asked how she liked the cake, she said she loved it. More fundamental than chocolate cake was the variety of ways Penny conveyed to Mary that she was not good enough for her son.

Since she was not good enough, Penny kept her at a distance. When she came into their home, Mary realized that this would not change. She had done everything she could to create harmony in the relationship and nothing was working; worse, it was creating spiritual havoc on Mary.

Mary went to their pastor, at the time Father Anthony Creech, who gave her some wonderful advice. **"I want you to begin to concentrate on the cross of Christ, and on what God did there for you and Penny. As time passes, you'll focus less and less on what she did to you." Caregiving for Your Loved Ones p. 154**

This is the way to freedom. First accepting that the Spirit works amid challenging circumstances and second to concentrate on the cross. We are all sinners and as Christians our only recourse is to the Cross. Mary began the long walk of healing. As she said, there were, "no lightning bolts streaking across the night sky." **Ibid p.154**

There was a dawning of understanding and empathy. She began to understand her very complicated mother-in-law. "I gained a new perspective on God's transforming power to heal."

In prayer, step by tiny step, I retraced the long path of Penny's childhood. I felt her fear as she pressed the covers against her ears, shutting out her parents' angry voices. **Ibid p.155**

I let myself feel the pain of the girl with thick, blonde hair, growing up without the handsome father she adored . . . I understood Penny's abandonment as written pleas to her tall, lanky husband went unanswered. The little girl deserted by her father was to raise her own son without his. **Ibid p. 155**

This rejection of father and husband drove Penny to take fierce, desperate control of everyone and everything in her life. She resolved to never be dependent on anyone for her welfare, a goal she achieved until her last years. But like sticky tentacles, her need for protective control crept beyond her own life to those around her. **Ibid p. 156**

From this God-given perspective Mary writes: Into my recognition of these facts and feelings God poured a new love. Penny's need for control would not change, and it didn't matter. Jesus alone was in control and because of Him I could simply let go. I could stare straight into space and understand and love even more.

> My spirit soared one afternoon as I introduced Penny to a nurse who was there to check her blood pressure. Penny smiled up at me, then turned to the stranger. "We have someone real special here," she announced. "Her name is Mary."

Ibid, p. 159

Mary learned a key lesson: if you pray for one who you are in conflict with, you don't hate them, and God has an opportunity to enable you to love them.

Somehow in Penny's tortured mind she was able to see Mary as worth loving. Mary with the Lord's help had put herself and her past with Penny behind her. She would experience healing and wholeness in Christ.

> *"Place My cross between you and the past, my child. I will bring healing, and make you whole again."*
> *"Even in this, Lord?"*
> *"Even in this."*

Ibid, p. 159

Mary's insight in "**letting the cross become the center of your caregiving relationship, not all the pain you felt for so long. And when the cross is truly at the center, everything is made new**, Now begins the exciting opportunity of allowing Christ to love your relative through you." **Loved Ones, p. 158**

Though this is written for caregivers it is applicable to today's hurting people and how as Christians are we going to love God and our neighbor.

In the post-Christian era Christ, has been forgotten, and chaos reigns. Children die of drugs, or violence, dialogue has become diatribe, and institutions have become shells of their former selves with no substance.

We as Christians are called to love God with all our heart, mind, and our neighbor as ourselves. Bob once said in a letter to Jacob "we are our neighbor in many ways." It can be done by putting the cross in the center of our lives. It becomes a bridge to loving God and neighbor.

Mary continues, "Now begins the exciting opportunity of allowing Christ to love your relative through you." **Ibid p. 158**

If I have learned anything as a Christian, it is I cannot do anything without Christ. Looking at the news, the entertainment, and the many casual cruelties that happen in this world.

It is easy to become cynical and hard. However, we can let Christ love others through us, the impossible becomes possible, difficult but possible.

Mary reminds us that after healing of a relationship, we still have memories:

"Did he give me amnesia? No. If I chose to, I could still wallow in the old pain. I chose not to. Instead, I consciously worked on seeing first the cross, then Penney. Jesus loved her enough to create her, then give his life for her—just as He did for me. What love! With that example and focus, releasing the past became easier." **Ibid p. 158**

The cross helped me understand and forgive my stepfather. To look at his life one can see the tragedy of poverty and abuse of his childhood, his unfortunate first marriage, the frustrations he felt with work, and the fear of change that stopped his emotional, social, and economic growth and development. This helped me to forgive him and to pray for him daily.

There is so much pain and brokenness in the world at large and in our own lives. The cross as described by Mary gives us a way out. It allows us to love God and to ask him to love others through us. Only as we love our neighbor can we love God and bring wholeness to ourselves and those around us.

These insights did not come without struggle for Bob and Mary nor anyone else. Mary writes in the devotional, *The Triumph of Tears*, they made it through faith, love, perseverance, and tears.

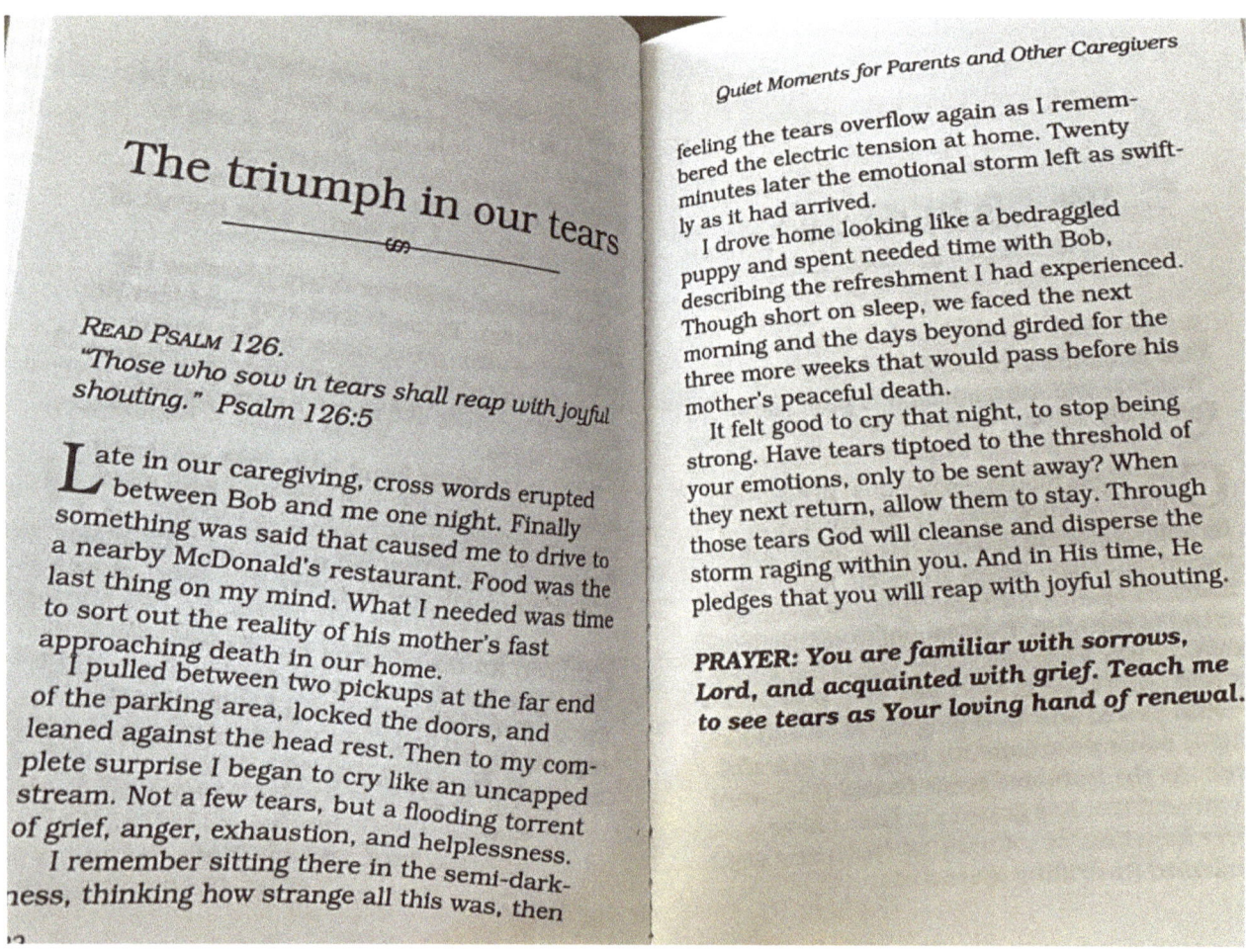

JOURNEY TO ORTHODOXY

I can honestly say that I do not recall hearing the whole account of how Bob and Mary came to the Orthodox Church.

Bob wrote to Jacob the following in their correspondence.

> We found our about St. Paul in 1992, through reading Fr. Peter Gillquist's book on Becoming Orthodox, and then looking for an Orthodox church in the yellow pages of the telephone directory. Our Chrismation was in 1994 at Pascha. What a joyous time. We

Letter 5, Bob's Answer to Jacob, 2011

The same information is conveyed and expanded upon in Mary's account. Rather than being given the whole panoramic view Jacob and I were offered a bite-sized account that we could digest.

The most complete account authored by Mary of their faith journey is in Virginia Nieuwsma's wonderful book, **Our Heart's True Home, pp 165-176, A Time to Listen, A Time to Hear.**

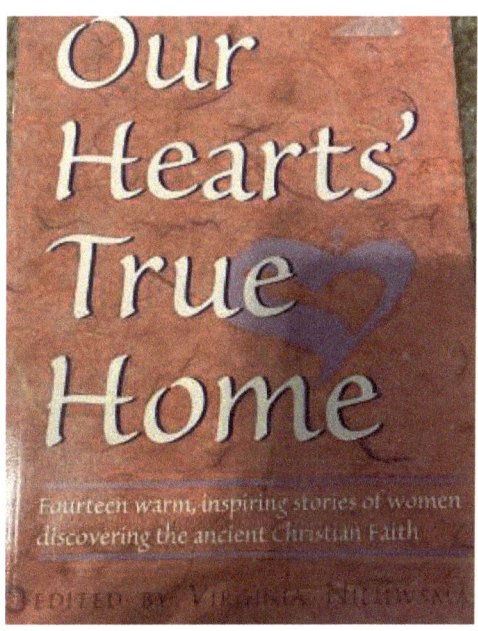

Mary had always felt the call of God and had been attracted to liturgical worship. They were nominally raised Scotch Presbyterian and had ancestors on the Mayflower. As Mary's mother said, "Our ancestors came to America to get away from that sort of thing." **Ibid p. 167**

She longed to worship him and felt His presence most deeply in those churches. She would as a young child walk into the Catholic church and sit and enjoy the "the blue candles and the statue of Christ above the altar." As she grew she continued to visit the church. **Ibid p. 168**

When she entered Stanford Nursing School in San Francisco a Campus Crusade group visited her dorm and she gave her life to Christ. This found expression in morning and evening prayer.

Mary found Grace Episcopal on Taylor Street met her needs for "majestic liturgy and more Bible reading than I heard before in one church." It was a perfect compromise for her and her Presbyterian Family. Mary was confirmed by Bishop James Pike two years later. **Ibid p. 169**

Mary was grateful for the place of the Episcopal Church in her life. It was a solace to her through the tragedies of her divorce, the loss of Christopher. It was also where Bob and Mary spent the first 27 years of their marriage. **Ibid p. 169**

In the 1990s people were looking for a faith that would not change. The Episcopal Church had changed, as did the Catholic. The Catholic Church of 1995 was not the Catholic Church of 1960. It had separated itself from the Orthodox Church in 1054 and until 1960 was still unique in that it had attempted to stay true to its core doctrine.

This was true until Vatican II changed the order of the Mass, stripped the Roman church of its sacred pictures and statues, turned the altars to west to face the people rather than east to anticipate Christ's Resurrection. Bob and Mary were amid a movement of people looking for Orthodoxy, and fortunately for them they were able to find it.

They began their search in earnest with a stable foundation to build a life on. They knew what the church should be and once was, and now they tried to find it.

As Bob and Mary moved, they looked for traditional Episcopal Churches and found shelter with Father Anthony Creech Holy Trinity Episcopal Church in Spokane, Washington. Knowing that they would be moving to Western Washington to be near their grandchildren, he advised them that they could do three things:

1. Find a traditional Episcopal Church, which was becoming more difficult.
2. Become Catholic.
3. Investigate the Orthodox Church.

Ibid p.170.

When they moved to Marysville, they attended the local Episcopal Church for about a year as they began to explore Orthodoxy. They continued to teach Sunday school. This search became more imperative after reading Father Peter Gilquist's book, **<u>Becoming Orthodox</u>**.

Bob consulted the Yellow Pages and found Saint Paul's Orthodox Church and contacted Father James Bernstein. Bob and Mary spoke with Father James and two days later a package arrived from him along with Father James's pamphlet titled "Orthodoxy: Jewish and Christian," which discussed Father James's conversion from Judaism to Christianity.

Saint Thomas More Catholic Church provided a temporary home for Saint Paul's, and it was there in a tiny chapel that they first experienced Orthodox Vespers **(p. 171)**.

They began an intense exploration of Orthodoxy by subscribing to *Again* magazine and reaching out to Deacon Ray Zell. To their amazement they received a kind reply **(p. 172)**.

While they were exploring Orthodoxy, Bob and Mary remained committed to their Episcopal Church Parish duties. They continued to go to Orthodox Vespers and absorbed Orthodoxy.

As 1992 ended they had the opportunity to attend Christmas Liturgy, as it fell on a weekday. They realized that they had found what they were looking for, a home for their souls and spirits.

They began to attend Saint Paul's consistently and wrapped up their commitments to the Episcopal Church.
Ibid p.173

"Six months after attending their first Christmas Day Divine Liturgy, they began regular, Sunday worship at Saint Paul's, and became catechumens a few weeks later."
Ibid p.173

In the ten months that followed they attended the weekly catechism offered by Father James and Kh. Martha at their home along with "a dozen or so other seekers."
Ibid p.173

In this warm environment they learned that "the Church's adherence to apostolic teaching and doctrinal purity, struggling always with cultural accommodation and innovation. We marveled that Orthodox Christians believe exactly what the church has taught since its first century beginnings."
Ibid p.17

Mary writes in an inscribed copy of **Caregiving to Loved Ones**, to Father James:

> **To Dear, Dear, Father James, Bonnie, and the Parish of Saint Paul Orthodox Church.**
>
> **Your friendship and warm welcome, have meant more than you will ever know. You have brought light and joy to our journey to Orthodoxy.**
>
> **In His Love,**
> **Mary and Bob**

This lovely little note captures succinctly the relationship that Bob and Mary had with Father James and Matushka Bonnie as well as the joy they felt in their journey to Orthodoxy. It was not one way, though. They brought light and joy to all they encountered.

> Property of Fr. A. James Bornstein
>
> To our dear Fr. James, Bonnie and the parish of St. Paul's Orthodox Church. Your friendship and warm welcome have meant more than you will ever know! You have brought light and joy to our journey to Orthodoxy.
>
> In His love,
> Mary and Bob

Cornerstones of Church and Lives

These two pictures look ordinary. A man in a beard is getting ready to set in place the cornerstone to Saint Paul's Orthodox Church. The other stone is the usual dedication. That is the purpose of the cornerstone, to commemorate the building of the church. Underneath the cornerstone was put a plastic box that contained the names of those who were members of Saint Paul's.

Like the last lines in Mary's dedication the pictures are a foreshadowing of the cornerstones of the church they helped build. This was done through their complete dedication to God, the church, and the community.

Age in our culture is seen as something to be avoided at any cost. The media promotes a youth culture centered on health and beauty and being perpetually young.

The realities of age, death, and eternal life are avoided or discounted. A well-lived life is a constant party, with interest and imitation of celebrities as the norms and standards of conduct, style, and behavior.

Those who are older are often discounted, ignored, dismissed, and their views not considered important. If one viewed the Armstrongs this way, they would be mistaken. They were not at the end of their lives but at the height of their powers. While I seemingly met them in the autumn of their lives, it was summer according to God's eternity, and they were at the apex of their spiritual maturity.

Bob and Mary would have been sources of wisdom, love, and active and invaluable members to any congregation. Divorce, loss of a child, and intense caregiving created understanding and empathy for those who experienced loss and pain and compassion for those who were suffering.

Their countercultural life of walking with faith and love with Christ, each other, and with all, to see everything as the providence of God for their good and growth, bore fruit. The fruit was the palatable love of Christ within the church for God and each other.

In God's eyes they were in the prime of their lives. Their eyes and feet were firmly set on their walk with Christ to the Kingdom of God. As they had walked with Christopher together to the Kingdom, they would walk with the people of Saint Paul's as far as they could until the completion of their own journey.

What some saw as an aged, retired couple, God saw as a couple prepared by their experience to be faithful servants, Sunday School Teachers, caregivers, empathetic listeners, and most of all a couple who radiated love to all.

Their legacy of love, kindness, and empathy would continue to hold the community of Saint Paul's in God's embrace as they took up the Armstrongs' mantle of lovingkindness after they completed their journey.

How They did It

Bob and Mary were Chrismated (Confirmed) on Holy Saturday 1994, the eve of the holiest day for all Christians, Pascha/Easter. Both found their heart's true home. Here was the church unchanged since its beginnings, which was a contrast from what they had experienced. **Ibid p. 174**

In Orthodoxy they found the fullness of the faith. The grace of God was present strongly in their lives during their Christian pilgrimage. It became measurably more full and powerful after they entered the Orthodoxy. The beauty that touched Mary so deeply is described in her words:

Always new and the same, the majestic, ancient, liturgy at once echoes and answers every cry of my soul, and I am lost in adoring worship for the Lord who has so loved me. With overflowing heart, I listen for his voice; at last, I hear. **Ibid p.176**

Reading her words again reminds me of what I love about the Orthodox faith. When one enters a local Orthodox Church, they are aware they have entered the Kingdom of God. The icons are of Christ and the saints remind us they are ever-present and a constant encouragement to live in union with God and gain Heaven.

"We are surrounded by so great a cloud of witnesses, let us also lay aside every weight and the sin that clings so closely, and let us run with perseverance the race that is set before us, looking to Jesus the pioneer and perfecter of our faith." (Hebrews 12:1-2).

The centerpiece of the Orthodox Churches is the Divine Liturgy. This is where Christ's death and triumph over death is celebrated and remembered each Sunday. In receiving Christ in communion, we gain union with him to overcome the many passions and tempests that assail us. We also are given the grace to be conformed to his image and to do what he asks us to do. Which is:

Love the Lord Your God with all your heart and with all your soul and all your strength. The second is this: Love your neighbor as yourself. There is no commandment greater than these.
Mark 12:30-31

Mary writes a key line on page 172, "We discovered a church nurtured by the Holy Spirit, **not only through desperate persecution, but through faithful everyday lives of people.**" In their faithful everyday lives Bob and Mary bore Christ in themselves and brought His presence to all who knew them. **Our Hearts True Home, p. 172**

Scenes from the Liturgy the Great Entrance and the Homily.

Joining Their Lives to Others

Often one thinks that to serve God they need to do some great deed. Often the will of God is found in the person who is right in front of us, and the Armstrongs were not afraid to join their lives to others no matter how they appeared, their personality, or what they were experiencing in their lives.

Bob and Mary were called to love God with their whole heart and their neighbor as themselves and they did. One of the ways they did this was as Saint Seraphim of Sarov encouraged us all to "acquire the Spirit of Peace and a thousand souls around you will by saved." Many fractured and troubled people came to Christ through the love and peace that flowed through Bob and Mary.

I know I did. In 1995 I met Bob and Mary at Saint Paul's, and over the next twenty years they brought order and beauty into my life. Life was never the same—Thank God!

Light-Intersecting Roads

I remember riding in the car when I was nine on I-5 south toward Puyallup to visit an aunt and uncle. On the right side we pass a small Russian Orthodox Church with its signature onion domes. I always wondered what kind of church it was and why the domes. Later I became Orthodox and learned the domes were stylized flames that gave the light of Christ to all who come.

In high school I found a movie about Czar Nicholas II. It was a short black and white movie that can now be viewed on YouTube. Then I had to thread it in the projector. I was fascinated because this man was the last emperor of Russia. The film showed him in church and with family.

I soon looked him up and read about his faith and the tragic fate of him and his family. Through all of this I grew more interested in the Orthodox Church and realized the connection of that small church to him. Czar Nicholas and his family would soon be canonized saints, and the impact of their lives, death and canonization would have a profound effect on my spiritual life. In reading about them I learned about the Orthodox Faith and Orthodox Saints who later would inspire me with their faith and courage.

However I soon realized that it was time to make a choice. The Orthodox Church can be quite ethnic, and while I was prepared to change my faith, I was not Russian and could not change my culture and did not know the language. Fortunately, I met a Romanian Orthodox teacher at City University.

She recommended Saint Paul's Orthodox Church because it was an English-speaking church full of converts from various traditions. The first time I went, I was completely lost in a strange new world. I had no idea what to do.

A tall, thin, gray-haired man greeted me. My first impression of him was of a displaced Episcopalian, but who was I but a displaced Catholic? We were all displaced looking for the fullness of the faith. Father James was a former member of Jews for Jesus.

Bob kindly gave me a tour of the church, how to light a candle, where to stand, and later I would meet his lovely wife, Mary. I stayed for the service and continued to return. I knew I was in the right place because I sensed the presence of God, and I began to know the Armstrongs.

When I was with them I felt the warmth of heart that I felt as a child going with my grandmother to Mass.

Entering the Light of Orthodoxy

Twenty-seven years after Christopher's repose. Our paths converged in the Orthodox Church.

After attending for about six months, I asked to become a catechumen. I was a catechumen for about two years and Bob and Mary became my godparents. I chose Bob and Mary because the light of Christ was in them. I found the warmth of God after so many years of searching.

In 1995 I was invited to their house and was immersed in the hospitality of their home. The first three impressions I observed upon entering were peace, prayer, and order. It reflected their values and lives.

The home was imbued with their values that had seen them through trial, tragedies, and joys. I could now see what a home with God and love for Him at the center looks like.

I was Chrismated December 24, 1995, at Saint Paul's Orthodox Church, by Father James Bernstein. I joined my dear godparents officially on their pilgrimage. Chrismation was just the beginning of learning the life of faith. To learn it one must live it, and I was privileged to begin living it in their company, and we would walk together in faith and love for the next twenty years.

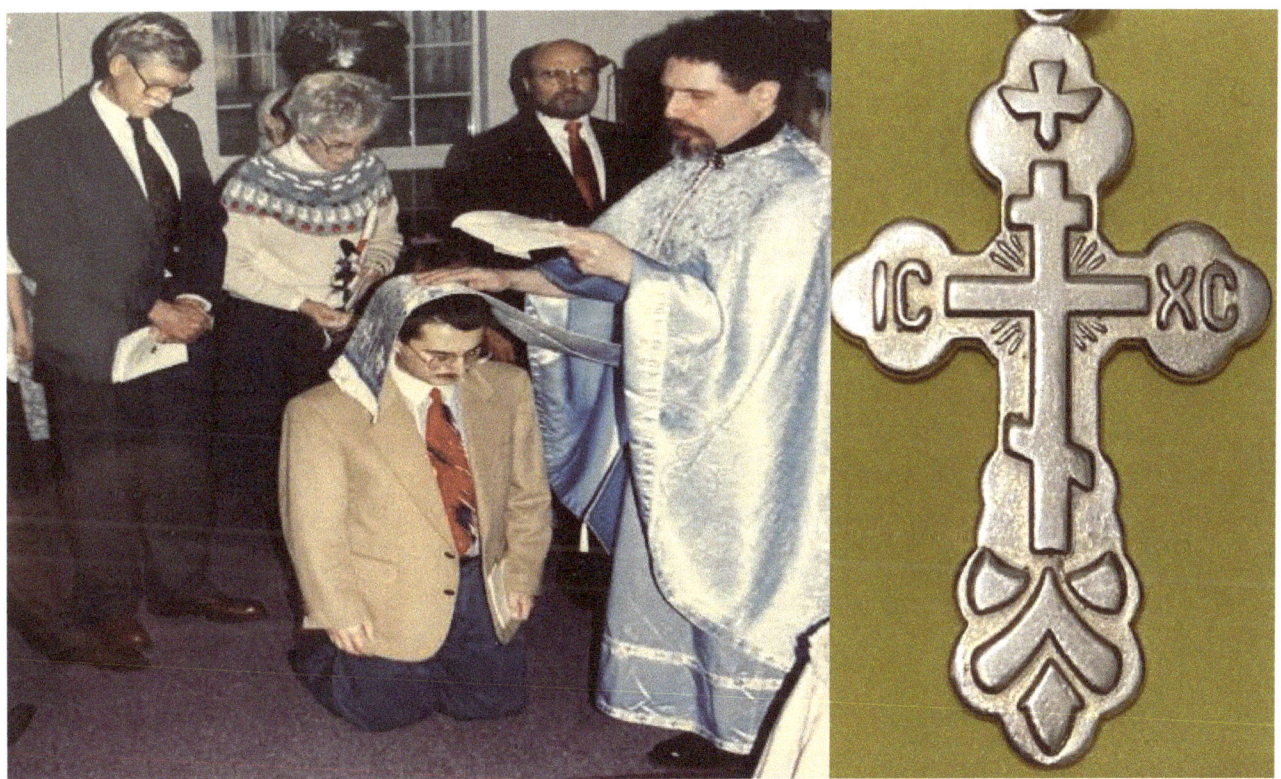

I chose the Saint Olga cross. I liked the symbol of the Holy Spirit and had always been fascinated by Russian history and the Orthodox Church.

Nineteen years later, in 2013, I would marry my wife, Olga, who is Russian Orthodox.

In their home and church God would continue to knit my inmost core together into the man I was meant to be.

Mary said that the more I received Holy Communion the more I would change. I did not understand this fully then and could not articulate what she meant until now.

Throughout His time on earth Christ healed by touching those who were suffering from blindness, those who were deaf, demon-possessed, raising the dead, and leprosy.

Leprosy in ancient culture was considered the result of sin and those afflicted with it were hated, exiled, beaten, and cast out.

Leprosy in biblical and modern times was a living death sentence. Lepers were kept away from those who were healthy out of fear of contagion physically and spiritually. A modern example is the former leper colony in Molokai, Hawaii. Like those in ancient Israel they were put in isolation without any means of support and were feared and despised by the general population.

Matthew 8:1–4 is the account of a bold leper. He said to Christ, "Lord, if you are willing you can make me clean." He was saying if it is your will (God's will), you can heal me.

Jesus did something that was unheard of at that time; he reached out, touched him, and spoke. "I am willing, Be Clean." Christ God reached out and touched a man with leprosy and said, be clean.

This scripture reminds me of the love of God for all who are disfigured internally or externally by sin and feel isolated. God reaches out and says, "be clean, be healed, be whole."

The more I received Holy Communion the more I would change. Mary was right because "holy communion is the place where we touch Christ, and He touches us." **Fr. Stavros Akrotriianakis**

To recieve Holy Communion is an opportunity to say each time like the leper, "Lord, if you are willing you can heal me." He then reaches out and touches us with his Holy Body and Blood and says, "I am willing, Be Clean."

Over time the body and blood of Christ changed and healed me. I became clean, healed, and whole.

Getting to Know Bob and Mary

Although nature and nurture have great influence, so does choice, and as I got to know Bob and Mary, I saw a way forward to become who I could be in Christ rather than who I was through circumstances of birth or home life, and I chose to walk with them on the path they were on.

The great grace I was given when I became Orthodox Christian was having Bob and Mary as godparents who modeled and lived a different life where love ruled. I drew near them and in doing so I drew near to God and His grace, and this changed my life.

Bob and Mary were never without each other. In the home, church, visiting relatives and friends, it was always as if they signed their emails to me, "US."

They leaned on each and supported one another. Together they listened to God to show them the next steps in their lives.

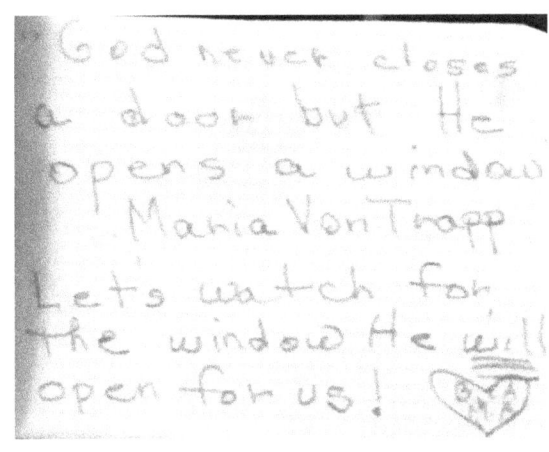

Order and Beauty

God designed everything with an internal beauty and order. When we follow that order by loving Christ, we can become participants in creating beauty with him just as Adam and Eve before the Fall.

However, with the Fall man sinned and the order disrupted man's ability to participate with Him in creating beauty.

This led to man being the cause of disorder; this is called sin. To overcome sin, we need to love Christ and let His love animate our lives and love our neighbor. Bob and Mary lived this in their daily life.

Everything we do has an internal order. Secular people may not recognize this, but it too is designed by God.

The model is the same for everything. Mary and Bob lived this model and structured their lives around it. Mary did this in her nursing career and in taking care of Bob. She ensured he received enough rest, made sure he got his vitamins, and when ill steps were taken that restored him to health.

Bob took care of Mary. In letter six to Jacob he wrote, "If I can help Mary in some way, I put that as a top priority." He made sure to lighten her load by doing the dishes after Mary had prepared the meals. Taking items to the post office, going to the printer, and having copies made for the scrapbooks.

The goal was to keep each other healthy and productive and in doing these tasks they were able to achieve this.

Bluntly, my life was in disorder, and I needed to be around people who lived a life of beauty and order daily and consistently to bring order to it.

Bob Steps In—Guiding Principles

Now there was a window of opportunity to make a new beginning in my life. They knew of the legacy of my stepfather, that I needed a strong, kind, Christian man in my life to mentor me on how the life of faith is lived. The need met the solution, and Bob was it.

"Love one another with brotherly affection; outdo one another in showing honor. Never flag in zeal, be aglow with the Spirit, serve the Lord. Rejoice in your hope, be patient in tribulation, be constant in prayer. Contribute to the needs of saints, practice hospitality."
Romans 12:10-13

Bob was the opposite of my stepfather in his nature and how he was nurtured. The absence of his father was a tender wound, but thanks to the loving support of his mother and extended family, he was allowed and encouraged to participate in all activities that would strengthen him in body, mind, and soul. In a very real sense, he built his life as a man of his own. Bob was a builder of men.

In all things Bob and Mary mutually agreed how to do this, and Bob took the forefront of building in me by word, deed, and example what a faithful Christian, strong man, with strong inner core who knows who he is and who he belongs to and lives God's will with his daily life.

This is a long statement, but these are the areas that needed repair and to mature. In order to live a life that God called me to live. They will be repeated when applicable further in the narrative.

Mary took the supporting role, and thanks to twenty years of love and prayers, I changed from a shy, intensely insecure, withdrawn, and fearful man to one of faith. I started to grow and draw near to God and to others in faith and love. The journey toward God's light and warmth had begun. There was a way out of the box. Together Bob and Mary put me in order through the love and grace of God.

The Builder of Men Begins His Work

Bob was a builder of men. A key element was work. One of the first memories and lessons was working with Bob retrieving railroad ties. Bob loved railroad ties, and when he came to my house one time and saw them, he asked my mom if he could buy them. They made a deal, and he made an appointment to come and pick them up with my help.

John recalls that he and Bob would work together. One time Bob got some free tubs that were later to move dirt from under a house. They would go for walks and kept a keen eye out for promising sights. One day they found an abandoned fishery that had some great wood beams. Bob put them in the back of the truck. He loved good wood and always had a vision for how he could use it.

I would continue the tradition of walking and working with Bob and the first lesson left me exhausted and curious.

Our railroad ties were in brambles, and I dreaded to help pull them out. I also thought mistakenly that I could outwork Bob because he was a senior citizen. It was a foolish assumption. The list of things that I did not know of Bob was long. I did not know that he had worked hard all his life. I did not know that he had trained young men in the past to look for railroad ties. I did not know he was an athlete as a young man and that he was stronger than he looked, and I did not know the value of a plan, his thermos, a long-sleeved work shirt, gloves, and a good meal to power him. I was about to learn it by watching him retrieve the railroad ties.

He came up with a plan and together we pulled about ten railroad ties out of the brambles. We then put them in Matt's old truck and transported them to their house. I was exhausted but he was as fresh as when he started. I was curious, and he said that he paced himself when he did a task and drank water. That was enough of an answer for the moment but it left much out. The reality is he was prepared not only for the task and would walk beside me teaching me the faith by example, strengthening my body and helping on the path of being a Christian and a man.

We then took them to his house and unloaded them and later they became an edge for his driveway with motion sensor lights so that visitors would be able to see their path.

Bob worked with me, spoke, and treated me kindly, with courtesy and respect. I was able to learn from a man for the first time. He also taught me to be prepared to work when an opportunity presents itself.

The wood was the opportunity. A responsible and industrious man looks for opportunities, and when they are discovered, plans and then works to carry them out. This lesson would be repeated many times over the years. He and I dug dry wells, cut bushes, mowed lawns, and lent a set of hands to building the raised garden beds.

I have used this lesson in my life most especially when I began to take risks, trusting in the light of Christ to make a plan, and pray that God's will be done.

The raised garden beds demonstrated the foresight and thought of the Armstrongs. Bob and Mary were senior citizens though they did not act like it. They wanted raised gardens so they would not have to bend so much and could sit on the ledge of the garden. This was brilliant. The raised gardens extended the years they could garden as they aged.

The lesson is to make accommodations to be able to do the activities you love. My accommodation in the future would be to relocate to Las Vegas and start my life as a teacher and become independent.

Bob's Physical Strength and Lessons

Bob in his younger years worked in hard jobs as a young man, and part of his normal routine always included exercise. He was a man from California who swam in the ocean and ran to keep in shape. The results of this were lifelong strength well into old age.

Looking at Bob you would see a tall, thin, angular man. His clothing and gentle kindness hid a man who not only had strength of character but of heart and body as well.

I saw this strength as we were chopping wood. I was having difficulty with a piece of wood that I could not split. I tried different angles and positions on the wood but did not find the sweet spot. Bob came out and I explained to him the problem with the wood.

He took the ax, eyed the wood, and swung. The wood was split beautifully. John recalls that Bob and he would cut many cords of raw wood together and would often have to split it. They would then stack it so it would be dry to use at the Lake Arrowhead house during the winter.

A standard, full cord of wood is a volume of 128 cubic feet, measured as a pile eight feet long, four feet high, and four feet wide. A full cord can weigh up to 5,000 pounds. Wikipedia

Photo from internet

His swing was beautiful, graceful, involved the whole body, and was the result of hours of practice. No wonder the troublesome piece of wood was done with such ease.

The thought flashed through my mind how Abraham Lincoln must have looked when he chopped a log. Like Lincoln's, this beautiful swing was the result of lots of practice and not obtained in that one moment.

A Lesson Learned—Back to the Present

Fast forward to 2023, eight years after their repose. I went back to my home state of Washington to write this book and stayed with my sister and brother-in-law who heat their house using a wood stove. The house is cold in the morning if a fire is not started in the stove.

They were going on a moose hunt, and he asked me if I wanted to learn how to light a fire. I don't like cold, so I immediately said yes. He and my sister are avid hunters, so lighting a fire is second nature. It was new learning to me.

He showed me how to create a base, use fire starter for a flame, then small pieces of kindling to build the flame, increasing gradually with bigger pieces of wood while adjusting the damper for air flow.

My first strategy was to keep it going and not have to start it in the morning, but Bob was right about sloth, and sleep spoiled the plan. I then awoke to a cold house. I was really motivated to start a fire and step by step I was able to build one.

Once the fire started, I watched it carefully. I went to the woodpile and collected pieces that would fit easily. Some were awkward. I thought, what would Bob do? I started by using an ax and making the larger pieces smaller. Surprisingly after some sloppy attempts, I found my rhythm with the ax. The reason was that if a piece of wood is too heavy or awkward, I could hurt myself and damage the equipment.

Next, I needed to prepare for the week. I made kindling and set it all up so that it would be ready for me. I gathered bark and toothpick sizes of wood in addition to kindling. It rests on a bark tray ready to go.

Prepared Wood   *Small Kindling*   *Large kindling*   *Beginning Fire*   *Mature Fire*

I realized I was thinking like Bob and organizing my work so that I would be ready not just for tomorrow but until my sister and brother-in-law returned from hunting.

The values of the lesson are still the same: nothing worth having comes easy. Everything of worth and value comes with desire or need, planning, effort, and execution as well as the blessing of God. This is true when I first worked with Bob and now.

This allows one to participate with God by listening to him, creating a plan, and completing it. Bob could not have guessed as he chopped wood, built a deck, put in a dry well, or turned a yard into a miniature paradise, what the future would hold, and these mundane tasks would be the building blocks of building a callow young man into the man he could be in Christ.

Time to Talk and Work

Work time was our time to talk. This was therapy for me, and I desperately needed to talk to a man that I could trust. My stepfather and I did not have long talks, and talking to Bob was needed to heal and overcome the issues raised by my stepfather. This act of listening was an act of love and love would rid me of those issues that had shaped me.

He listened attentively to what was said, observed unobtrusively and always had the right words at the right time. He also did not give long answers. They were a few words that I could hang onto and apply. A lesson I learned: if you want people to remember what you said, make it short, to the point, and memorable.

A Man of Many Names

Bob was a man of many names. To the youth in our church, he was, depending on the parent, Mr. Armstrong or Bob. To John and Matt, he was Pop. One day in 1968 Bob, John, and Matt went for a walk and they were wondering what to call him. Mr. Armstrong was too formal, they had a dad so they agreed that would not work; they finally decided on Pop. To me he was Bob. More importantly he was my godfather, he was more like a father to me, it is because of him and Mary that from the age of thirty-two to present I have led with God's help a faith-filled and joyful life.

Model Mentor—A Man is Humble

Bob was always kind, patient, honest and a brilliant teacher. He taught by planting seeds. He knew I loved him, and he knew I was thoughtful so he would give me something to think about. I would meditate on the latest morsel and then we would explore it.

There was only one day my feelings got hurt, and it was when he said I was being slothful. He was right. I was slothful. I probably would have taken it better if it was not front-loaded so directly. I honestly did not expect it. I was upset and close to tears. What happened next had never happened to me in my life.

He apologized. He said, "I forgot you were not Bob but you." This was a revelation. I had never had a man of his stature apologize to me. I was stunned. Here was a man I admired more than anyone, apologizing for correctly telling me the truth but was not quite ready for it.

This was an example of humility that I have always kept close to my heart so that I can remember to practice it. I had never seen it. My stepfather would never admit wrong, much less apologize. Yet Bob was sensitive and made the effort to get me back on my feet. As a man learns to hear and accept truth he grows in mind and inner strength; as he learns humility he grows in heart.

In my twenty-five years of teaching, I learned that the most powerful thing an adult can do for a child is to apologize. I remembered how it restored me and the relationship with Bob and how if I practice it with those I offend, it can restore relationships with them as well.

Bob showed by example healthy Christian manhood by living it. Thanks to his example and the twenty years of love and prayers I was able to stand upright and leave the defensive fearful crouch of my childhood.

Photo courtesy of Jacob McGinnis
This is the Bob we all knew and loved in his work clothes
keeping the church in order and beauty.

The Pilgrimage of Work and the Fellowship of the Task

Bob explains his love for home projects in the above quotation. The first reason is one must keep one's home going. Then he gets into the creative aspect that he so enjoyed modifying and innovating, using the materials that he had on hand if he did not have the piece that he needed. He loved the challenge and keeping the home going, and the process itself that gave him an outlet for creativity coupled with practicality. He was also frugal and if he could save money by doing it himself it was that much sweeter.

> My hobbies and interests center around home improvement projects, also known as do-it-yourself work to keep things running where you live. This is oft-times a challenge to see how you may be able to modify or innovate with the materials you have on hand. I have always enjoyed being a "handyman", some times for money, but more often for fun or the challenge. I wish I could find more time to read, but I am able to shoehorn in short breaks here and there. (Many busy people always keep a book, article, etc, close-at-hand) I believe that keeping your home is good stewardship.

Generations Project, Letter 4, Jacob McGinnis

Bob was self-taught and I believe trained himself by reading books on home repairs, through trial-and-error and learning as he went. Bob retired at sixty-two and by the time this letter was written Bob had been retired for twenty years, and at eighty-two, at that point, he had a lot of experience.

He and I did many projects over the years. We also incorporated the prayer before any task. This was the next lesson. Along with measure twice and cut once was to begin all things with prayer.

Bob was always organized. Where I would just want to dig, he would lay out the tools and then explain how to start. I would dig until I was tired, and he would never get tired and finish. I began to internalize his lessons.

Plan, be organized, measure twice, cut once. After we would say grace, have a meal and I would go home. This was a lesson to me: always begin with prayer, plan the project, set up the equipment, and proceed with the task. This is a plan for every task of life and for life itself.

He learned how to use tools and create wonderful things on his own. Every house he and Mary lived in was made more beautiful through his efforts.

A Palace Fit for Chickens

One of the projects that I missed was the McGinnis chicken coop. The McGinnis family raised chickens, and the old coop had fallen into disrepair and needed to be rebuilt. Bob, who loved a challenge, jumped at the chance. These pictures of the replacement demonstrate Bob's love of building community and character, while working on a project.

Bob made sure to include godson Olaf, an experienced construction worker, along for the fun. The picture of Bob with knee pads on, long sleeve work shirt, tool in hand, looking at an upper beam surrounded by the McGinnis boys show Bob's love of building and bringing others into the process.

Jacob McGinnis, who was a godson and was there when the Palace was built, writes touchingly of the impact of Bob and Mary upon his life:

Photos courtesy of Jacob McGinnis

Letter from Jacob

Jacob kindly allowed me to use the letters from his project that he exchanged with Bob. These letters formed the basis of the Generations Project for school. I asked him for a few paragraphs about the role Bob and Mary played in his life.

> It is hard to summarize how amazingly loving and important Bob and Mary were to me, our family, and to our whole parish. They truly were like an extra pair of grandparents to everyone that knew them. They will always be my example of how an Orthodox Christian should behave. Despite whatever was happening in their own lives, they were always overflowing with love and joy, and spread it to all those around them.
>
> I could not have asked for more saintly godparents than Bob and Mary. Every time I saw them, they greeted me as though we had not seen each other for years. They were constantly engaged in my interests and shared in my love of birds. I would get weekly updates from Mary about the hummingbirds that frequented their yard. If she noticed their activity was starting to drop off, she made sure to inform me, and ask for help in attracting them back to their yard. In fact, this was the last thing we ever talked about in person before she was admitted to the hospital.
>
> I have very fond memories from my childhood visits with Bob and Mary at their house in Marysville. I remember helping Bob stack firewood, rake leaves, mow the lawn, or combat the blackberry bushes that bordered their backyard. At the time, I viewed these tasks as annoying chores that I just wanted to complete as quickly as possible, so that I could get inside and get dinner. Nowadays, I would give anything to be able to mow the lawn or rake with Bob one last time.
>
> Another memory from spending a weekend at Bob and Mary's is of them discussing the importance and power of the Jesus Prayer with me and my brothers. They made sure that we all said it together that night during our evening prayers. Later that night, I woke up around one or two o'clock in the morning to a train whistling in the distance. I sat up in bed, while looking out the window at the town in the distance when I, for the first time that I can remember, said the Jesus Prayer by myself, over and over again, until I fell back asleep.
>
> "Trust in God with all your heart, and do not exalt your own wisdom. In all your ways know wisdom, that she may cut a straight path for you; and your foot will not stumble." Proverbs 3:5-6, the verse Bob and Mary wrote in the front of the Bible they gave me in 2008.
>
> Jacob McGinnis
> November 14, 2023

In these five paragraphs we find the path that Bob and Mary followed and shared with a generation of people of all ages at Saint Paul the Apostle Orthodox Church.

First, they were examples of how an Orthodox Christian should behave. No matter what was happening in their lives they were overflowing with love and joy and spreading it to others around them.

Second, most of us regarded them as saints because they walked and lived the faith. They were genuinely glad to see Jacob and interested in what interested him. They had a phenomenal memory and asked detailed questions about his interests in birds, and Mary talked about her interest in hummingbirds. This open-hearted love and interest in others created a bond between Bob and Mary and Jacob. They had the gifts of memory, of welcome, interest, and commonality that was shared with all who loved and knew them.

Third, here we see Bob the builder of men inviting Jacob to the fellowship of the task. Like most of us he did not like it at first. We just wanted to complete the task and dive into Mary's dinner. Like him we all wish we could go back and do one more task with Bob.

Fourth, the power of prayer. This was a gift that all of us who were godchildren got to at one time or another pray with Bob and Mary, particularly the Jesus prayer, which means so much to Orthodox Christians and is part of our prayer rule.

Fifth, "Trust in God with all your heart, and do not exalt your own wisdom. In all your ways know wisdom, that she may cut a straight path for you; and your foot will not stumble." Proverbs 3:5-6. This is the path of how to navigate through life. Trusting in God and allowing his Holy Spirit to cut a straight path through the brambles and twisted paths of this world.

Putting Away Childish Things

Working with Bob was a joy and created new memories, displacing the old ones of working for my stepfather. In working with Bob, a new man was being built. I was becoming stronger in body, mind, and spirit while helping add beauty to Fair Havens. The fellowship of the task was building me into the man I hoped to become. A strong man in body with mind and heart centered in Christ.

Photo by Mary Armstrong
Working on the raised gardens.

Our Adventures Along the Way

Bob and I had some adventures while working. One time Bob decided that a tree needed to be pruned. The branches were only accessible from the roof of the house. He and I went up to the roof with an electric tree trimmer on a long pole.

Bob, who was then in his mid-to-late seventies, thrust the device onto the limbs with me behind him holding his waist as ballast so he/we would not fall over the side of the roof. I was praying for two things, the first that Mary wouldn't catch us on the roof and the second that we would not fall.

Together we conquered the battle of the branches. Bob said I had a puckish, playful, and mischievous sense of humor, and I could not help but think we were imitating Saint George slaying the dragon or Don Quixote chasing windmills.

Men About Town

Bob and I walked everywhere. I learned it is the best way to meet people and create community. We often went to the neighbors' to get eggs. It was near their home down a small alley. It was a tiny remnant of old Marysville, where neighbors lived close together and your neighbor might have a few chickens. It was always great to go there because my ancestors were pioneers of Marysville, and to see this was a link to my history.

We also went to the Marysville co-op. It would only be a slight overrstatement that all the employees of Dunn Lumber greeted Bob like Norm on *Cheers*. They all knew his name because of all the work he did around the house.

The co-op was a classic mom-and-pop operation. Most of the employees had worked their entire lives there, along with their children. They knew all the customers and it was a hub of the local community. I would go in with Bob and then explore the store.

It was a link to a history that might have been mine if things had been different and if I had been raised there.

Bob and Mary's youngest son, Matthew, and Tony, their grandson, was interred at the Marysville Catholic Cemetery, which was not far from the Marysville co-op.

We would have a moment of silence and then Bob would kiss his fingertips, touch the headstones with his finger. Then he would say, "God Bless, you son. God Bless you, dear Tony." Their memory was fresh and green with Mary and Bob.

Here was someone who felt the pain of the loss of his loved ones. He honored their memory by going weekly to the grave. He and Mary never denied their pain or stopped talking to others about Matthew and Tony. This was something that allowed me to love, mourn, and talk about my stepsister, Bobette, and in time, visit her.

They lived their life loving God and their neighbor, and they trusted in the promise of seeing their departed ones in Heaven.

Bob's inner quiet and steadiness was both like a strong sequoia to Mary and a rock of stability to those who were blessed to know him. It was born in adverse circumstances and bore fruit of faith, hope, and love throughout his life.

Walking as the Measure of Time

I loved walking with Bob, and I learned to measure the passage of time in the number of steps. We walked from the co-op to the house quite often in the early days. One year Bob had a staph infection in his knee, and the infection did not leave his body.

Rather than stop walking he walked within his limits. When we once could walk from the co-op to the house, now we walked the cul-de-sac near Fair Havens. Often, we would go buy fresh eggs from a neighbor. Finally, when this became too much, we would walk with a cane or walker around the driveway, looking at the yard, the house, and the gardens that Bob and Mary continued to enjoy. No matter where we walked, we enjoyed each other's company, sometimes in silence and others in conversation.

This persistence of Bob is an example in life of his core belief that you never, never, quit. His physical walking was an example of his spiritual walk. He never quit, always reached his goal, and gained eternity with God.

Living Light—Godparents to Many

Courtesy Jacob McGinnis

Bob and Mary lived the Orthodox life and helped others live it as well. When Bob and Mary became godparents, they were involved with the lives of their godchildren. The Orthodox Church and their lives in the parish were the center of Bob and Mary's life.

They were active in each faith group they were a part of. Being involved in church and living it out in the world was part of their spiritual DNA.

Bob and Mary were active godparents as well. It is not known how many godchildren they had. The estimate ranged from eighty to one hundred. Each godchild could select a cross of their choice of up to $100. They would wear this cross as a confession of faith in Christ and protection from evil.

On their birthday they would be sent a birthday card, accompanied by a joyous, fun, loud rendition of "Happy Birthday." All looked forward to it. They would receive a name day card.

Life events were celebrated such a marriages, births, and anniversaries. Being a godparent for them was not a one-time event, but a commitment to that person to walk with them in their life of faith.

They were the busiest retired couple I have ever known and took time for the things that were important; their family, godchildren, and friends were their priority. These cards reflected this. They were carefully chosen, often handmade, with a positive message of love and faith.

A sampling of the cards

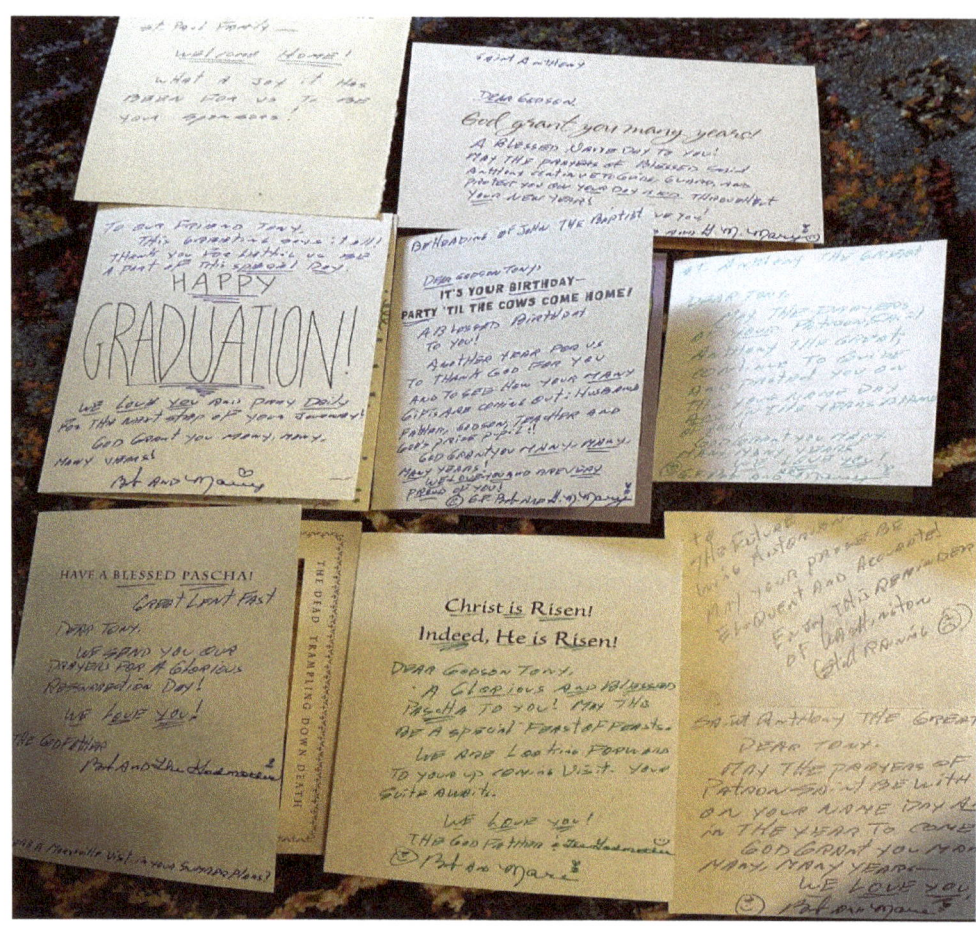

Messages from the Armstrongs

Going to Church

Bob and Mary used each minute to the max and everything was well-timed and organized, and going to church was no exception. In the Orthodox Church we are encouraged to prepare for Holy Communion. They did this every Sunday on the way to church. After the car was loaded with Sunday school supplies or food for coffee hour we would be on our way.

Mary would read the prayers before communion as well as the scripture and commentary for the day as well as a biography of the Saint on the way to the church.

Mary had a beautiful reading voice, and the thirty minutes to church passed quickly. We were ready for church upon our arrival.

Church Life

Bob and Mary's philosophy of service was, how can I help? They did what was asked of them to the best of their capacity. **Humility and love for neighbors were the hallmarks of their service to Christ.** The church is the body of Christ. Everyone has a role from the priest to the layman. Everything is done for Christ.

They were active members of Saint Paul's Orthodox Church. Each served where God as their talent led them. Mary was the facilitator of the prayer chain, taught Sunday school, and was part of the Women's Group.

Bob was a key figure on the parish council and a sounding board to the clergy. He was well-educated, spent a career working in personnel, astute politically, faithful to God and had great integrity. He had no guile or personal agenda and wanted the best result for everybody.

He would reach out to parishioners weekly and check in on them. He often invited them for lunch and in the breaking of bread Bob would listen to his guest. His listening was great, and conversations were a gift to his guests, and they left feeling refreshed and affirmed.

Mary ran the church prayer line. This is a tough job. No one knows the amount of pain someone is carrying inside. Mary was very empathetic and would not only take down the information and pass it to the prayer chain but listen and support the person making the request.

Men's Group

Bob was instrumental in founding the Men's Group, which began with morning prayer in church, and continued with, "The Best Breakfast for a Dollar," which was cream cheese and a bagel and reading a book about the faith, for example one of Saint Seraphim of Sarov.

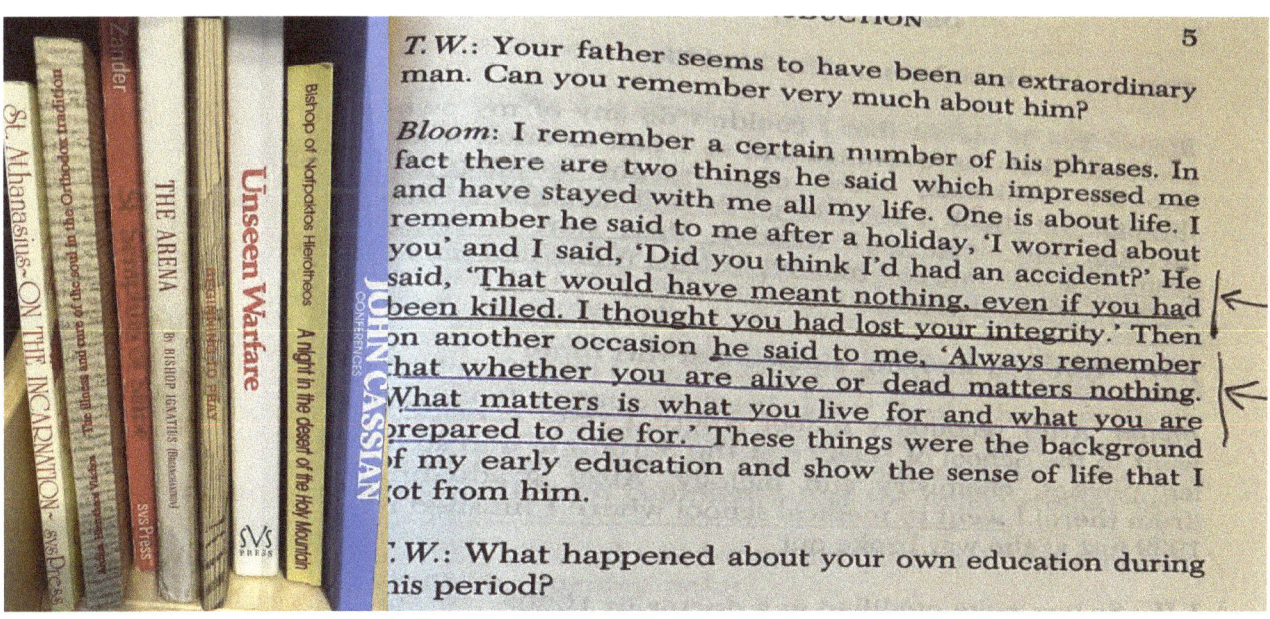

Bob's books that he used during Men's Group. His books are underlined.
The underlined portion above from Beginning to Pray reflects Bob's values.

These books would take years to read because as we read them, we discussed them. *On the Incarnation* by Saint Athanasius took three years, and it was one of the smaller books.

All of us were converts, and we had no context about the topics of the books. Father James helped us navigate our way through them.

In the Present—He Teaches Me Still

I recently ordered another copy of **On the Incarnation,** then I found the one Bob used. At first, I was reluctant to read it because of the underlining. I realized my prejudice against reading underlined books was stopping me from reading and being with Bob. Reading his underlined passages allowed me to follow his thinking. What a joy it was to sit with him again while I read this book. I am so grateful to have the set of books he used to reread them and feel again the presence of my dear godfather and continue to be taught by him.

ST Athanasius, On the Incarnation
Page 41.

Here is a page from the book with his underlines. Wonderful words from a great saint, underlined by the Servant of God Bob Armstrong.

Back to the Past

In Bob's life two themes can be observed. The first, a love for Christ, and the second, a love for his brothers and sisters.

Bob and Mary believed that this found expression in meeting people where they were at and walking with them on their journey.

The natural corollary to the Men's Group was Mountain Movers. This group of men helped families load belongings for parishioners who were moving from their current residence to the next. Prayer was combined with action and found its fruit in this group.

Bob and Mary were a vital part of these groups and attracted people to them, and their touch of kindness and grace was the touch of Christ.

They brought their gifts of time serving with the talents and grace that were given them and in doing so loved Christ and their neighbors in tangible ways.

Bathroom Monitor

While I am sure Bob did not want it, he did it. Saint Paul's youth were not angels, particularly the boys, and Bob had previous experience in another church with boys of a preceding generation with similar traits.

He knew boys in particular like to extend their break from church by playing in the bathroom. Years earlier in a previous church he caught two children making a fire.

These two had the fear of Bob put into them who in their case was a higher power in height, strength, and voice, and they did not repeat this behavior.

Bob monitored the bathroom at Saint Paul's, saving it from flooding and putting the same fear into another generation. The boys knew and loved Bob; they did not hold and grudge and became men of God in their own right.

Coffee Service—Hospitality

Over time I got to know Bob more by working with him in the church. At the time he was in charge of setting up the bookstore, which with my love of books was a natural fit. In addition, we made a huge pot of coffee for coffee hour.

This, like all things, Bob was done precisely and with a plan, and at a steady pace. The pot was put in the sink, filled with water, and coffee added. It was then put on a rolling cart along with the orange juice, then carefully and neatly put on a side table. It worked out well and was done efficiently and with taste.

When our group had coffee hour, we got the cutlery set up on the serving table, took down the chairs off the tables and prepared them for coffee hour.

When coffee hour was completed, we reversed the process and swept and mopped the floor. It all sounds very mundane, but it was an act of hospitality of the heart and body and was a blessing to those served and the servers.

As Bob grew older, he tended to focus on making the coffee and preparing the orange juice. This involved filling heavy coffee pots and urns, placing them on the cart and placing them in the hall. It was a routine that he loved. He was glad when the younger people took over his other duties and felt a sense of satisfaction that those ministries would continue.

Coffee Hour Duty

Celebrating Sofia's birthday
Courtesy of Jacob McGinnis

Consistency and commitment are rare qualities. Bob was there every Sunday participating in creating hospitality with this work. It was done so well that no one noticed, and that was what Bob wanted.

He knew his blessing was from God, whether it was noticed or not. Most of us want a "Well done." Bob was aiming with his quiet humility for a "Well done, good and faithful servant."

Bob and Mary celebrating with their brothers and sister in Christ

Sunday School—Passing the Faith to the Young

Mary's first-grade Sunday school teacher, Miss Bacon, would have been pleased at how well Mary listened to God and followed her words. Especially with Mary's passion for the religious education of the young. Her years working as a public health nurse and school nurse and raising four children gave her an understanding and empathy for the young, and she may not have said it in the same words, but her message to the students was that if you listen to God, He will hear you.

She was given a curriculum, and like all good teachers she used it as a guide but added meat to make it interesting to her students. She spent hours preparing and creating projects for the weekly lesson. Her special talent was making books that used the materials from the lesson and was something that the students could take home and share.

Photos Courtesy of Jacob McGinnis
And Muhleisen Families

She was a master teacher and taught Sunday school in various faith groups since 1968 and had thirty years of experience when she taught at Saint Paul's.

One day she asked me to watch her while she taught. I had recently had a teacher's evaluation and used that rubric as I watched her. She hit all the marks. What is more, the students hung on her words. They loved and adored her, and I know of a few of her former students who are listening to God and hearing Him.

Women's Group—Fellowship

Women's group was close to Mary's heart, and their hearts were close to her. In her days in the Protestant Church, she was a retreat and conference speaker. She knew that women needed other women for fellowship.

Bob and I would set up the hall getting chairs done and getting the space ready for them. Once that was done, Bob would let Mary know. The ladies would gather in the fellowship hall, and she would be in her element talking, laughing, and listening to those around her. I must admit even though I did not stay long after setting up for them I envied their fun. I was attracted to their joy. It was something that I as a man could learn from. Less earnestness and more laughter.

Photos Courtesy of Jacob McGinnis
And Muhleisen Families

The ladies also got together in one another's homes for informal get-togethers. I am not sure of the occasions, but they all looked like they enjoyed themselves.

Waiters—Humility Service

Bob and Mary clothed themselves with humility, and they were in deep cover. I don't think anyone knew about their families, their accomplishment. They knew them as Bob and Mary from Saint Paul's, which is exactly what they wanted.

Photo Courtesy Mary Armstrong

Bob looked at the following opportunity as living out the love of God by loving neighbor.

Saint Paul's sponsored a clergy retreat for the Deanery. Bob volunteered us to be waiters and servers of the gourmet dinner that the church put on for the priests and their wives of the Northwest Deanery. Here those who served were served.

The house was beautifully decorated, and the meal that was prepared looked excellent. The volunteer servers took the role seriously. The clergy felt treasured and comfortable enough to relax among themselves without worry knowing that this dinner was for them. The servers kept a distance and did not intrude in that precious space except to serve.

If the Son of God can leave Heaven and wash the feet of the apostles, then die on the cross for me, the very least I could do was to serve them who serve the liturgy that give us the body and blood of Christ. It was a good exercise in being a servant and watching Bob serve with such grace and class was a lesson in humility and what a servant looks like.

Looking back at this I remember the words that the priest says before we receive communion, "servant of God (Name) partakes of the Precious and All Holy Body and Blood of our Lord God and Savior Jesus Christ unto remission of sins and everlasting life."

It made me appreciate the clergy and realize that the pride in me needed to be purged so that I could live in union with Christ.

The Light of Fair Havens

Oliver Clement writes, *The transfiguration of the world requires creative contemplation, active love, the most heartrending personal compassion, and the ability to reinvent life. It is a question of giving human beings not only bread, but also beauty, opportunity, and celebration.* (Mother Maria Skobtsova, Essential Writings, P.11)

God has designed everything to be beautiful and has an order to it. When we follow that order by loving Christ, we become participants with him in creation just like Adam and Eve.

Overall Routine

Bob and Mary built their lives on the framework of routine. It provided the structure upon which they gained their spiritual, physical, and mental sustenance. It had specific times to rise, pray, work physically and mentally. The Orthodox Church was an integral part of their lives with attendance of Vespers on Saturday and liturgy on Sunday.

Daily Routine

A normal daily routine would consist of rising, scripture, reading, morning prayer, and breakfast.

Bob would take a cup of coffee up to Mary as she was getting ready for the day. Bob and I both used the downstairs bathroom. I often played a game trying to get to the laundry room steps near the bathroom door while he shaved, his hearing was so good that he heard me every time. Then we would chat.

Mary would sometimes prepare breakfast. If not she would begin the day taking coffee to her home office and work. Here she edited books, contributed articles, worked on the prayer line, wrote cards to family, friends, and godchildren, as well as answered her email and phone calls

Most of the time Bob prepared oatmeal topped with fruit for us. We would meet in the afternoon for lunch.

Bob and I in town would say the prayer before any task. We would then work on one of our projects with the same intensity until lunch.

Lunch was taken separately. Bob would prepare tuna salad sandwiches and something for Mary. Bob would offer thanks to God for the day and the meal. Mary would return to her desk depending how much work needed to be done or would go outside and tend the flowers and garden.

After lunch we would put the placemats, napkins, in their place, wash dishes and go back to work.

This would continue until around four, and Mary would prepare a meal. While the meal was being prepared, we would say the evening prayers as well as the prayers of thanksgiving for the meal.

Supper, the last meal was served later in the evening. It was served on beautiful trays in the den. We then watched a news show.

After the dishes were complete, we would say goodnight.

This routine seldom varied. We may go to breakfast, or guests would come for the evening meal.

The daily routine was almost monastic in pattern and rhythm. My wife confirmed this and said that the house felt peaceful and holy. Everything was prayerful, orderly, and beautiful. The outer order reflected the inner order of their lives.

We need structure. The military provided structure and I thrived. The daily bell schedule of the school and routines of the day provided structure to teacher and students. Structure is key to life in work and retirements.

Their structure was inundated with prayer and purposeful work and had a natural rhythm that gave meaning to the day and its tasks.

Beauty

Fair Havens was a place for "creative contemplation and active love"; it was a place of beauty, where compassion, kindness, humor, and empathy were served with a good meal. It was a place that let God change one's heart and become new.

Bob and Mary made their home a place that all wanted to visit. After painting several rooms, I smile when I think of Mary describing paint as beautiful and thick. I now know what she meant. They painted the entire living room and furnished it with pieces from both of their lives, making it their own.

Mary created beauty in all places lived. First, she loved light. Fair Havens was situated to receive light. The windows in the kitchen were alight with sunshine in the morning and the front shared it in the afternoon. Both were from southern California and cherished seeing the sun, particularly during the winter.

When winter came Mary made sure the lights were on so that Bob would not feel light-deprived, which is common in northwest Washington. Mary had wonderful taste and decorated the home using the best of both their furniture. The living room had comfortable stuffed couches and chairs always with accent pillows to welcome visitors. The kitchen, though small, had a hanging cupboard with glass doors so you could view what was in it. Inside there was a variety of vintage dishes and two silver wedding bells with 1968 on them.

Bob's joy was the outside and he made many improvements. The railroad ties framed the sidewalk and motion lights were installed to guide family and friends into and out of the house at night.

Mary loved flowers and the inside and outside of the house reflected this. They had four planters hanging from the edge at the front of the house. Each was a little garden unto itself. The gardens in each of her homes were places she could go to reconnect with nature and her Creator. She was able to meditate on the psalms, enjoy the air, and decompress. Years before when her son Matt was young and had the flu, she brought some flowers in.

"Together they marveled at the fragile green stems supporting dainty blue labella. Four delicate petals, each less than a quarter of an inch, embraced the pure white centers. We wondered at the giant pansy, admiring the reds and purples that flowed from its compact yellow center." **Quiet Moments p.94-95**

This time relaxed and refreshed Matt and Mary. In those moments they shared in the wonder of God's artistic creation in nature, and they gave themselves "time to hear the Creator's voice. Nature was a way to be in beauty and conversation and be present with each other." **Quiet Moments p. 95**

The flower on the deck, yard, and in the hanging pots were an homage to the memory of her mother. Roses grew and bloomed red, pink, and fragrant in the cool Northwest sun and were often brought in and placed in a small vase before an icon and crystal statue of the Mother of God.

This is the statue that Mary put a rose and candle before. It now sits in my prayer corner.

Roses, light and whimsy on the deck.

She gave roses not only to her earthly mother but her heavenly one as well. The back yard was a place of many family celebrations and summer meals served on the deck.

Going into the side yard there were raised gardens that produced fruits and vegetables that Mary prepared for meals. As one traveled to the deck there was a spacious yard with more pots and beautiful rose plants that Mary used to nurture tenderly.

Mary said you could create beauty with what you have, even a tin can and some flowers. I remembered this when I discovered a lone carnation separated from its stem. I recalled Mary's wisdom about a tin can and flower and placed the carnation in the jar.

Mary was right—you can create beauty from a flower and jar. Looking back, the deeper lesson is that beauty was created by a humble jar and damaged flower. It is a good analogy for what God does to us if we let him. He creates beauty where there is damage and fills us with good things.

Mary created beauty and places of peace using what she had. One of the things she had was sunlight that shone beautifully on the trees. Saint Francis is crowned with reflected light, and the clay bull frog and roses appear to appreciate its warmth. Everything blended harmoniously.

> # Blossoming in life's shadows
>
> READ PSALM 17:6-8.
> *"Hide me in the shadow of Thy wings."*
> Psalm 17:8b
>
> One Sunday last summer my husband and I went to church, then treated ourselves to an afternoon of backyard gardening. We trimmed spent iris blooms, sprayed roses, weeded flower beds, and watered the pots of pink and white petunias.
>
> All afternoon the fourteen pine trees in our yard created broad splashes of sun and shade. But this didn't seem to bother the plants at all. Roses, petunias, marigolds, and snapdragons thrived in the bright sun. In the cool shadows nearby other plants flourished with equal abandon: waxy white begonias, dainty impatiens, graceful columbine.
>
> Wherever they were rooted, God provided continuous growth for each plant. Maybe you're feeling a little like a shade plant today, and wonder if you're growing at all. Like rosebushes, most of us equate growth with comfort and warmth. We forget that God delights to use every event, every condition of our lives to produce the blossoms He desires.
>
> Today's verse implores the Lord to hide its writer in the shadow of His wings. There the psalmist knows he will be in his heavenly Father's embrace. Parenting brings difficult choices and decisions, and it helps to thank God for those shadowy times. Through them He mysteriously draws us to Himself, cultivating spiritual growth as varied and beautiful as flowers on a hot summer day. What special challenge do you face today?
>
> **PRAYER: *Father, thank You for allowing the circumstances that cause me to grow. By faith I accept them, and their spiritual harvest as yet hidden from my sight.***

Quiet Moments for Parents and Other Caregivers pp 54-55

In the devotion titled <u>*Blossoming in Life's Shadow,*</u> Mary writes about a summer day that she and Bob had the opportunity to "treat ourselves to an afternoon of backyard gardening." They "trimmed spent iris blooms, sprayed roses, weeded flower beds, and watered the pots of pink and white petunias."

While some like me would rather be on the deck reading a book, or others watching TV or doing an outdoor sport, Bob and Mary found joy in working in their garden. What they were doing was what Adam and Eve did in tending the garden of Eden. It was their way to meditate with God in His creation.

Using the fourteen pine trees that provide shadow and sun and life to different types of plants as analogies for our walk with God—sometimes we are in the sun and sometimes we are in the shade, but the sun are the good times and the shade the tough times. "God delights to use every event, every condition, to produce the blossom he desires."

Bob and Mary experienced both conditions in their lives. The light and shade were not merely meant to allow one to survive but to thrive and grow. No one wants to suffer or lose those they love through death and tragedy.

No one wants cigarette butts shot at them. The question is how does one respond to it. I think it comes down to trusting in God's providence. In my case I learned what and who I did not want to become, and I spent my life looking for it. It was a pilgrimage.

God would give me light for the journey and when I took a wrong turn allow me to go to the dark, but his love never changed. What changed was my direction.

The goal was to live in union with God and bear the fruits of His Spirit.

The church and their home became a place of recovery for myself from the toxicity of my childhood home and stepfather.

He led me to the Orthodox Church and to two dear people who were well-prepared by Him to show myself and others how to live in Christ. The more I participated in the services of the church, particularly the liturgy, the more His light illumined me.

Carefully the accumulated rust of years of fear and mistrust were removed and replaced with the grace of being open to love and mercy. It is an ongoing work and healing and is never finished, and life gets better because of it.

I look back at the photographs of their home and see the fireplace alight and the cozy couches in front of them. The armchair by the fire and the rocking chair close by. It was a safe place for conversation, laughter, and healing.

When I was over for dinner the table was set beautifully and the meal prepared with care. One of Mary's key priorities was her home: "Our home became my family's springboard into the world, undergirding all of us for whatever the day might bring." It was for the family and the numerous people who became family. **Caregiving p. 120**

Etiquette

Bob and Mary's dining room was my first classroom in etiquette. I had seldom been in a house that used place mats or cloth napkins with rings, nor had I seen silverware placed properly. These were lessons I was blessed to learn with kind souls.

Mary said she has seen all types of table manners over the years, so I felt free to make mistakes. I was used to eating at my desk or picking up fast food.

Table etiquette provides a structure and rhythm to a meal that is relaxing and allows one to enjoy conversation, appreciate the beauty and order of the table, and enjoy a wonderful meal.

The Gift of Listening and Conversation

I learned to converse and to express myself when I went with them to visit family and friends. I learned by watching them how to interact with others.

One of the gifts that Bob and Mary gave was the gift of listening and truly hearing what the person was saying with words and behind the words. Mary beautifully describes this almost lost art.

"Using two ears isn't enough. Gentle silence, a soft touch, a nod of the head, warm eye contact, and laughter are all a part of real listening." **Quiet Moments p. 64**

This gift was given to all who arrived at Fair Havens. During summer when the yard, garden and flowers were at their height, guests would come and sit outside amidst the beauty. Relaxed by the surroundings and their host the conversation would flow.

An example of this with a couple might look like this. Mary sensed that her goddaughter needed some time with her and invited her and her husband over for an afternoon. Bob and his godson would have their own conversations.

In separate areas both Mary and Bob would be sitting silently, eyes on their godchildren, letting them talk, listening to the content, and the emotion behind it.

They were present with them in each curve of the conversation, and when the flow of words stopped.

Photos Courtesy of Jacob McGinnis

Photos Courtesy of Jacob McGinnis

They would share their thoughts based on years of wisdom applied to similar circumstances.

Not all conversations, of course, were this intense, but their attentiveness to hear the thoughts and validate who was spoke by listening to them was greatly appreciated and cherished.

Bob and Mary in relaxed conversation with John and Lynn/Photos Courtesy of Muehleisen Family

Conversations like these were repeated thousands of times in various places over the twenty years I knew them and further back than that. They were the building blocks of friendships and community that spanned the years from one generation to the next, becoming not just their community but family.

They did this by always going in with a smile and ready to converse and listen. I spent several Thanksgivings with them at their son John's house. It was not hard to talk to the family or when their girls were small to play and laugh with them. It was the best environment to learn how to socialize.

When friends from the church would come for a meal, there was always good fellowship and I never heard a negative word about their guests.

They demonstrated that having an open heart, a kind countenance, a willingness to listen and not react but to interact led to a wonderful evening and created bonds of friendship that nurtured the soul.

Bob and Mary took the initiative in creating relationships with kindness. On Christmas every year Mary would make baskets for each of the neighbors and would go to their house and ring their bell.

Everyone knew the Armstrongs and eagerly anticipated the knock or ringing of the bell; this kind action created a community for them and their neighbors. The lesson was be kind and create kindness around you.

Over the years of witnessing and participating with them in their daily lives, I changed and started eating meals that had class and grace. Working with Bob digging holes and going to the neighbors with Christmas gifts—all of this was life-changing for me. I became more open to loving my neighbor.

Prayer and Theologians

The word *theologian* today means one who studies a course in theology and obtains a degree such as a Master of Divinity. This degree is required for Holy Orders.

The Orthodox have a different definition. Evagrius Ponticus writes:

"If you are a theologian, you truly pray. If you truly pray, you are a theologian."
Evagrius Ponticus

Saint Evagrius Ponticus definition of prayer according to David W Fagerberg is:

> *a "theologian is someone who has been shaped by the cooperative exercise of grace and ascetical submission, whose eyes can see after their light has been restored, whose heart wills only one thing, whose mind has changed, whose life has been reconnected to the source of life. This does not require a PhD; it requires a conversion of life."*

Father Boris Bobrinskoy shows what this looks like:

> *If "the one who prays is a theologian," it is because—we can say this very humbly—each one of us knows prayer in the Spirit. In moments of true prayer, the grace of the Holy Spirit in the heart of our being causes a longing, a desire, a cry for help, emotion before the beauty of the cosmos, or compassion for the suffering that surrounds us. The Holy Spirit introduces us to communion with the Son, Jesus Christ, in the mystery of the Incarnation—the debasement, humiliation, suffering, and death. He educates us to compassion, by making us suffer with the Lord.*

Prayer and Theologians Practiced

Bob and Mary according to Dr. Fagerberg and Father Bobrinskoy were theologians. They cooperated with God and submitted their lives to his love and will and were connected to the source of life. They experienced "moments of true prayer," and "compassion for the sufferings that surround us." They lived in communion with Christ in their joys and tragedies. This honed their compassion to an even greater degree for those of us who knew and loved them, and we knew that God heard them.

Mary had been drawn to prayer as a young girl. When she used to ride her bike, she would prop her bike and go into a Catholic church. When she was older, someone would ask where Mary was, and another would answer, "Probably praying." Mary could really listen to God and responded with prayer. Our Hearts True Home, p. 167-168

Prayer was their food and forte and through this ministry lives were changed. Mary ran the prayer chain. It was an active and vital ministry, comprised of volunteer members of the church who prayed for the multitude of needs for the parish and those in need. Mary took down the names and spread them to the team.

They had lists of their own that had hundreds of names on them. People were prayed for with intention that God would work in their lives to their specific needs and according to His will.

I observed Bob and Mary praying their prayer rule and using these lists while they prayed. The lists contained names, the issue, dates, and results. If a person reposed, they were moved to another list and prayer continued for their souls. The opportunity to pray for the individuals and community was a great blessing to Bob and Mary and those they prayed for.

In their room was a lovely prayer corner. It is an example of Mary creating beauty with items from their life together. A cherry chest proved to be a solid and attractive table. The icons were tasteful and the green chair was a good place to sit when needed. Here they would pray for those who asked them.

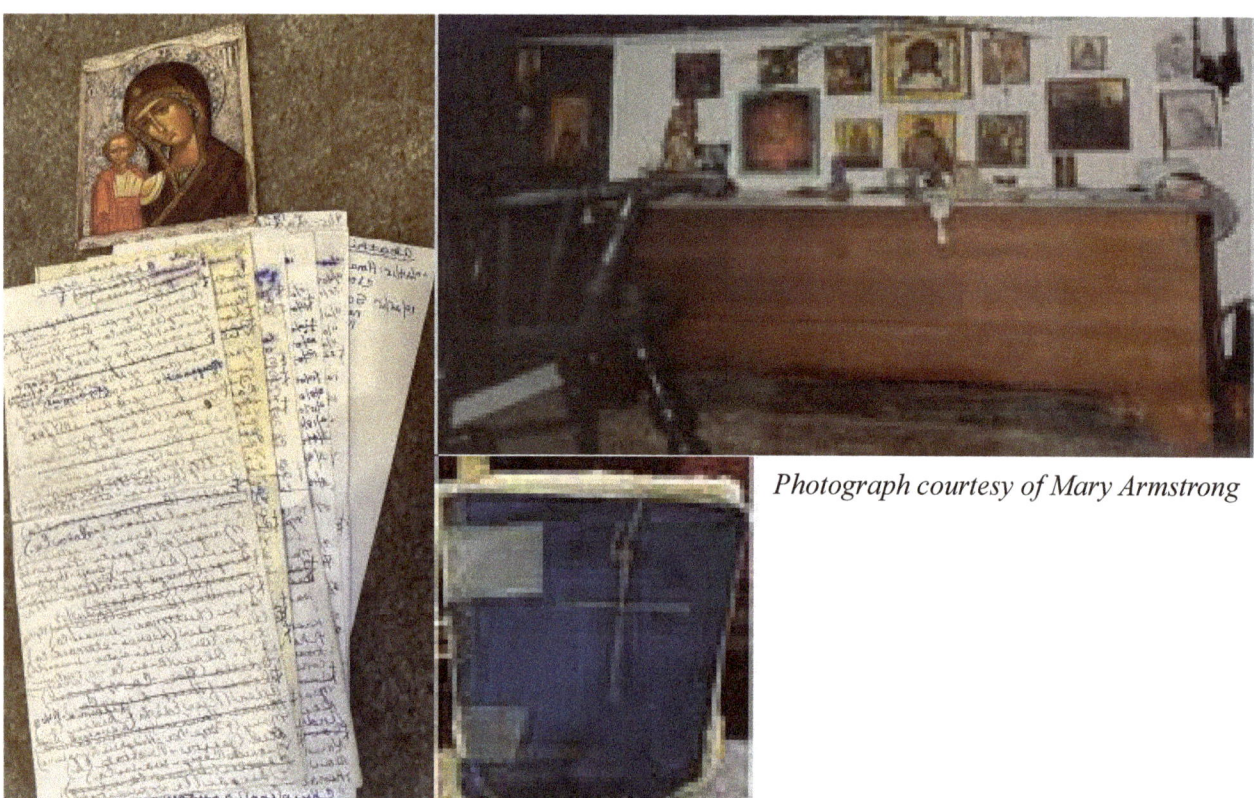

Photograph courtesy of Mary Armstrong

I have a portion of their prayer lists on recycled paper. It is only a small portion of the many prayers lists they used over the years. There are notations of what the person needed, the progress, and if the person reposed.

I read through them and most had cancer. She and Bob prayed not just for members of Saint Paul's but all who asked. Mary lost two sons to cancer, and had it herself in various forms, was praying for others with the same disease. The last entry is 10/25/15, a little less than a month before her repose.

They would say evening prayers before dinner. Bob would use his blue prayer book. He was thrifty and loved this book. It is worn out from use. He repaired it using tape, his bookmark was a piece or ribbon, and he would use a paperclip for prayers that he wanted to add to it. It is old and tattered, the pages shiny with age, and the tape barely holds it together. It rests on my prayer table, a reminder of the prayers and love of my dear godfather.

If you looked on Bob's wrist you would find an old worn prayer rope that he used to repeat the Jesus Prayer, Lord Jesus Christ Son of God, forgive me the sinner. Together they would say the familiar prayers. The Lord's Prayer, prayer for intercession of family, and then they would pray for the people, whose names were on small pieces of paper, and set them on the shelf in front of the kitchen window.

These were persons who had immediate needs and would be included in their daily petitions. They would pray for their children, grandchildren, their former spouses, extended family, and their church family. One could feel God's loving presence in that small kitchen.

I have over the years looked back at this area of my life. Gradually over time I realized that I needed to pray in my life. It is easy to go to church on Sunday, but the problem is there are six days until the next Sunday.

My beloved godfather was right. I tend to be slothful and lazy; however, I cannot fast from God for the six days between Sundays, and if I would work hard to stay in contact with those I love, the least I should do is work toward staying close to God during the week.

This means morning prayer, along with my prayer rope, and scripture reading, and going to Vigil or Vespers, along with weekly liturgies when available. Each person's prayer rule is different as mine is with Bob and Mary's, but it is what I can do now. It gives me the daily bread of Christ's presence.

Dinner in the Den

Dinner was often served on trays. Like all things Mary did, it was done with taste, beauty, and order. Each tray had a salt and pepper shaker, a cloth napkin, a salad fork, a dinner fork, and a knife.

The meal would be organized as well, a salad in a lovely bowl, butter in a dish, the main course plated and hot.

Grace was said and we would take our trays to the den and set them on wooden trays. The den was a small room with a TV lined with books from Bob's youth set in bookshelves built by him while he was in high school.

In the center of the den was a picture by Richard and Francis Hook, called, **Let the Children Come Unto Me.**

It was a large portrait and I asked about its history. They said it was a gift from a friend to remember Christopher. Seeing that little boy being embraced by Christ gave them comfort that Christopher was with Him. This portrait followed them through their various moves.

I had a connection with this picture as well. Early in my faith journey, I went to a religious bookstore and purchased it. I liked the many children surrounding Christ and saw myself in that boy that is close to Him. It gave me comfort to know that Christ loved me.

Bob would fit his long frame into a long and cozy chair. He was quiet and reflective. Mary would be on the couch in her comfortable house clothes which was often a red sweatshirt and jeans. Together we would watch McNeil and Lehrer on PBS, who I must admit tended to put me to sleep.

Photo courtesy of John Goddard

Mary would have her legendary large address book. I cannot adequately describe it. The first thing one noticed was the size. It looked like a notebook that had overeaten, and its mouth was permanently wide open ready for more crying, "Feed me."

Mary fed her beloved beast such treats as calendars, to do lists, and innumerable other things. It seemed to enjoy it and grew with the newest tidbit. While I could not detect an internal coherence, it was not mine to detect. She used it effectively and updated it often. Mary took our questions and wide-eyed wonder in stride and laughed with us.

Her hands and mind were always busy. If it was not her address book, it was knitting, and it was never about herself but always for someone else. It was her way to unwind and relax.

After we were finished eating, we would clear the dishes and Bob would wash them while watching the program on the small TV in the kitchen.

I was equally close to her. I adored and loved her. She was a force of nature and nurture who drew people to her through her real interest in their lives.

My time with Mary either between tasks where we would have a short pot of coffee or was after dinner in the den while Bob washed the dishes. He would turn on the TV in the kitchen and we would all follow the program.

While doing this we would chat about the days, what had been accomplished, how the scrapbooks were going. How the family was and how the garden was growing.

When the dishes were done, we said good night. They then retired at their own time, often with a bowl of popcorn. I often went to bed before them, though they were in their mid-to-late-sixties to their eighties when I knew them. I was always tired before them. Knowing how they lived their lives in their prime I am not surprised they were able to keep up their pace in their upper years.

Bob and Mary's marriage was an example of what makes a marriage work. It was grounded in faith, communication, compromise, and shared tasks and purpose.

Bob's humility can best be seen when he took the coffee to Mary. Mary loved coffee and would be busy working in her office. The coffee was a break for them to say a few words and provide a respite for her.

Meeting Those Closest to Me

MY MOTHER

My mom visited Bob and Mary and they had a couple wonderful visits. My mother was raised in Marysville, Washington, and is a member of the Regan family who were pioneers of Marysville. Her grandfather John Regan gave the land for the first schools and owned and operated a wood shingle business. She experienced poverty when her father lost the family business because he was too trusting and did not have a head for business and soon the family found itself in abject poverty when he passed in 1949 living in a converted chicken coup that was known in the neighborhood as the Regan's shack.

My mother in front of her home and childhood toys.

The place had electricity to put in to keep the chickens warm but it had no running water or indoor plumbing. Once a week they used a car to travel to a local stream and filled two ten-gallon milk cans for fresh water for drinking and cooking

They caught rainwater from the eaves of their house in fifty-gallon barrels. This was used for animals and washing clothes

(This picture taken December 21, 2023, of water going from the roof into a bucket shows how much water is produced during a rainy day.)

Washing clothes was done by heating water in a large pot. They put this in a washer machine with a wringer. They then used two galvanized tubs to ring the soap out of the clothes. Then they were hung on the clothesline, summer and winter.

Water used for animals and to irrigate when needed was hauled in galvanized tubs from a shallow well that my uncle had dug to the house in a cart.

To take a bath they would heat the water in a galvanized tub, then pour it into a portable bathtub and place it near the wood burning stove for heat as they bathed.

Fruits and vegetables were grown on the farm, and my grandmother canned them, and they were used throughout the year. My mother knew she was poor but never felt it.

My grandmother valued education and saw it as a way out of poverty for her children. All five of her children graduated and all five avoided poverty. Her children laid the foundation for the next generation's success.

My mother's life had moments of challenge, but this early experience gave her the persistence to overcome those challenges and to thrive.

Mary was impressed with her knowledge of history and her persistence. She said, "I like your mother." That meant a lot to me.

In 2023 Mom gave me her high school graduation ring, class of 1958. She wore this ring through my childhood and beyond. It was like the bouncing ball that landed on lyrics in the old musical cartoons. This ring was present in all the lyrics of my childhood. When I wear it, I reflect on her life and realize that the gift she gave me was the example of persistence and perseverance and how to never give up.

FUTURE FAMILY

In 2013 my godparents opened their home and hospitality to my beloved future wife and stepsons. Bob and Mary were extremely kind and generous. Their legendary energy was lower due to age and declining health; however, they rallied and gave my family a memorable time.

We went to BoonDockers and had wonderful breakfasts with lots of discussion. What I remember is how generous with their time and energy they were and how engaged they were with Olga and her sons. I also remember Olga telling me that she felt that the home was prayerful, quiet, peaceful, almost like a monastery. I am so grateful Bob and Mary met my family and prayed for us.

ERIC

The next friend I brought was Eric. I met Eric in high school. He was a refugee from Vietnam who is Chinese. His family had to flee Vietnam because of the communist takeover of the country. Together they worked to get every member of their family the education they would need for a successful life. Eric went into aerospace. In Eric Bob and Mary saw a person with drive, determination, and love and commitment for family along with incredible humility, all virtues that they and their family valued and appreciated. They always remembered him, and Eric never forgot them.

BUM

Bum is someone I admire deeply. He is what I strive to be. A faithful Christian, a strong man with a strong inner core who knows who he is and who he belongs to and is comfortable in his skin and lives God's will with his daily life.

Bum in the 1990s

When I met him, I was nowhere near this, and only as I entered my forties did I begin to see the seeds of those qualities in me. Now in my early sixties, because of the grace of God, I can say that they are there. That does not mean that I have made it or that I can be complacent. I am so grateful to God that they happened at all. As Christians we are in the long game and strive to become Christlike throughout our lives, until we reach Heaven.

Bum had them in his twenties, and he really impressed Bob and Mary. I loved watching them talk. In Bum I saw who I would like to be, interacting with love and faith with those who would help me to reach my goal.

I recently talked to Bum on the phone about Bob and Mary, and I thanked him for his role in my life. He said something to the effect that God brings us together to become more like Him. It affirmed the role Bob and Mary played in my life and reminded me that I am called to love others and be a part of their lives in a way only known to God.

JOHN

Bob and Mary met my dear friend John Villesvik. John and I went to elementary school together, but we were not close. I was as appealing as a feral cat. John, though, talked to me, and I used to go to his house and got to know his family. They were kind Presbyterians, and like the Armstrongs, provided a window into what a Christian home looked like.

We went to high school, and he was a competitive swimmer. He then went to WSU and graduated with a degree in architecture.

What was fascinating to me between these points was that he was a Big Brother from an early age to numerous Little Brothers and would mentor these young men until they were ready to launch their lives.

I saw him at a high school reunion, and we had a great visit. By that time, thanks to Bob and Mary and the kindness of God, I was well-launched, and the feral cat banished to the land of the past.

He posted beautiful pictures of his hikes in Washington. This was a lifelong passion. It was a place to meet God in His creation and to stay fit. John was fit. He was six feet, six inches tall, and all muscle.

I tried hiking with him, but I could not keep up. I later found out that not many could. I am five feet five, about the size of one of his legs, so we found other ways to fellowship.

John where he loved to be.

We would meet at Denny's, which he loved. I knew he had a career as a draftsman in an architecture firm and gave it up to work as a King County Corrections Officer in 1994.

I was curious why he made the change, and he said much like Bob he wanted to "build lives more than buildings." Here was a man of faith, going into a place that few want to enter, to those in need. He lived Matthew 25:36: "I was in prison, and you visited me." God changed lives through John and only God will know the full impact of his life upon the young people that he interacted with while they were incarcerated,

John was killed in a hiking accident on his beloved Mount Rainier May 24, 2019. He was mourned and loved by all who knew him. He was like Bob and Mary, an extraordinary person clothed with humility and living the light of God where he was placed and the person he was with. Losing him was almost as hard as losing the Armstrongs. I know that I joined the many that wept at his funeral.

Like Bob and Bum, John was a Christian and a man. He lived both fully and is a role model of what I aspire to. I know Bob, Mary, and John are together in Heaven.

Each of these men taught me something about how to be a man. I was a stranger, and you welcomed me. Eric invited me into his home and life to be part of his family when we were both young. Bum and John were models of what real Christian men look like. All three of them inspired me to keep going and become the man I am meant to be in Christ.

Scrapbooks

Mary was always goal-oriented and strove to use every minute wisely. This project was close to Mary's heart because she would be passing on the legacy of her family going back generations and transmitting that history to her children and grandchildren and their children.

All her skill of organization, the wisdom acquired in her eighty years of life, and her excellence as a writer were concentrated on the completion of this project.

This project took precedence over her writing and editing career, with the last fifteen years of her life dedicated to creating scrapbooks for each of the children and grandchildren.

The logistics were daunting. If my count is correct, at least ten books needed to be prepared. Bob would often go to Marysville Printing and have copies made for each of the ten books, and then the material had to be inserted.

Mary's high standards are reflected in the quality of the scrapbooks. This high quality can be seen in the pages she created earlier in this work. They are an archive of treasured memories and the values that had sustained the family.

Mary worked on them through the challenges of aging, illness, and family tragedy. She may have paused her work, but she always resumed it with vigor.

She barely made it in time. After what she called her blow out, which I believe was a perforation of her colon, she sensed that her health was declining and increased her efforts to finish.

She finished them and gathered the family and presented them to each member of her family. This project was her magnum opus, great work, and she reposed not long after.

Celebration in the Light

> ### Celebration: homemade therapy
>
> READ PROVERBS 17:17-28.
> *"A joyful heart is good medicine."*
> Proverbs 17:22a
>
> "Hey, what's all this for?" Our son, a new Marine recruit, eyed the carmel icing swirled over his favorite chocolate cake.
> "We're celebrating!"
> "What's going on?"
> "You're going into the Marines," his Dad explained as I placed the cake in front of him. "And are we proud!"
> "All right! Is this German chocolate?"
> The time sped by as I cut slices and scooped vanilla ice cream onto waiting plates. As we enjoyed it, everyone at the table focused on stories about Matt. Despite his upcoming departure from home he devoured three helpings, laughed with us, and even shared some of his feelings as Boot Camp neared. It was a celebration we've never forgotten.
> Today's reading does more than recommend laughter. The Lord also makes clear its therapeutic value, akin to good medicine. What's coming up for someone in your family? Could you uncover an excuse for a celebration, however small in scope? It doesn't take much: a bouquet of fresh daisies delivered with a hug, a special dessert, homemade signs and streamers, a favorite meal, a cluster of balloons. Why not try your hand at working a family celebration into the days ahead? It costs next to nothing, and the memories last forever.
>
> PRAYER: *Open my eyes, Lord, to the family milestones all around me. Teach me to crown the art of homemaking with the art of celebration.*

Quiet Moments for Parents and Caregivers, pp. 76-77

Anyone who met and knew the Armstrongs, knew their joyful hearts. In this devotion about celebration Mary makes it clear that laughter is good medicine. It is a chance to be together and to rejoice with each other.

Matthew was about to go to Marine Boot Camp. Even when the training was challenging, he would have the memory of this celebration and the love of family to cheer him on.

Boot Camp was a challenge; Matt and his buddies would keep their spirits up by celebrating and toasting the other with their canteen for each day that they had made it.

The Orthodox Church provided them with numerous opportunities such as name days—feast days in addition to a birthday, baptisms, and weddings. As Mary writes in the piece, the occasion can be anything, it does not cost much, and it affirms the love one has for the other person, and it is something we can all do.

Mary Armstrong, Scrapbook
Courtesy, John Goddard

The holidays began in October with the annual pumpkin party and Harvest Party in the garage. The car was pulled out, tarps laid down, a heater was employed to take the chill off and tools set out for the event.

John and Rita arrived with their three girls and Matt and Laurie with their two boys. The music was the nonstop conversation of adults and children. Ordinary pumpkins transformed from gourds to smiling jack-o-lanterns. Bob and Mary and the family thrived in this joyously noisy chaos.

The Thanksgivings that I remember were at John and Rita's. The family would gather at their lovely home each with a dish to offer. The table was sumptuous, and the kids were excited to be together with cousins. There was a keen sense of joy and thanks for all of God's blessings.

Christmas

Christmas was a special time of the year. They were remarkably organized and their preparation monumental. Shopping began just after Thanksgiving. Preparation of gifts took the rest of the month and most of December. Gift wrap, bows, cards, everything that was needed to wrap gifts was organized and made ready. Each gift was chosen with care, wrapped beautifully, and the name tag often had a small message.

This was not done for five or six gifts but maybe a hundred. In addition, gifts were sent to family and friends near and far and were prepared with meticulous care and quality.

Looking at family photo albums, I see the Christmases past; I see a little boy unwrapping a big package. I was clearly excited and was happy to get the gift that I must have wanted. The adults talked and the kids played.

Something seemed lacking though. I think the unanswered question was, why we were doing this? There were feeling of "I should be happy, but what is the reason?"

What was lacking was the reason "that Christ was born to raise the image that had fallen, which means to restore our beauty as living icons radiant with His holiness."
LeMaster, Philip, Rev.

Pictured Christmas 1968 from top to bottom, Bobette, Kerry, and myself. This is one of The few pictures of us together. Bobette would repose January 9, 1969.

It became real for me when I celebrated Christmas with the Armstrongs. After the Nativity liturgy we would go through the house putting the baby Jesus in the Nativity creches throughout the house. This tradition was done by the youngest member of the house and I was it, even though I knew Bob and Mary were young at heart. In doing this my heart became childlike, and the incarnation touched me in an intimate and tangible way.

Then I knew why the adults did not look happy and why the toys soon became old. It was because the babe in the manger was not in my childhood home. He was in the Armstrongs' home, and I understood Christmas as the time when Christ has come so that we may become who we are meant to be in Him. This gift never tarnishes and is always fresh and gives the joy of God to all who hang onto Him.

Christ the light of the World is born! Glorify Him!

Then we would load the van with gifts and visit the family. I was so grateful to be included in the family holidays. It was a joyful time to see the children's happiness. It is hard to believe that those children are adults and have children of their own.

Christmas was joyous I had never seen or participated in, so beautiful, full of kindness, and grace. I treasure the memories and hold them closely to my heart.

The only time this routine was interrupted was the Christmas of 2008. I literally arrived from Las Vegas to Marysville just ahead of the biggest snowstorm that the Northwest had seen in years.

Bob and Mary picked me up from the Tulalip Inn, where the bus dropped me off. As we were driving home the snow began to fall and it kept falling. We arrived before it worsened.

Roads were icy and treacherous, and the roads were soon closed. We were officially snowbound. The church sent an email to all not to risk coming, and we would celebrate the Christmas Liturgy when the roads were safer.

A roaring fire with Maggie the cat on my lap.
Photos by Mary Armstrong

It was a phenomenal Christmas. The home was cozy, and I sat in the chair with a cat on my lap and read before the fire. We talked and laughed. Bob and Mary made sure to call family and friends and the exchange of gifts was deferred until the roads cleared.

This was the spot where the cat and I would sit by the fire. I would read and she would sleep. I felt secure and happy in Bob and Mary's home. It was a haven of peace.

Bob and I went and dug out the driveway. It was nice to be together and good to be outside. The scenery was beautiful. It was quiet, no traffic sounds. Mary was both a memory maker and keeper. As Bob and I worked she took pictures and used them to make a mini scrapbook which I treasure.

Every year Bob and Mary worked together to send out a Christmas card to family and friends. In addition to church, Sunday school, coffee preparation, scrapbooking, birthday greetings, visiting children and grandchildren, godchildren, editing, shopping, and projects around the house and outside, they found the time to compose their annual Christmas card.

Below is the last Christmas card they would work on. Life was becoming more challenging. Mary was fighting cancer but it was not the focus with either of them. Instead, their thoughts were finding time in the day listening to Christ. In it, Mary asks, can we turn off the unceasing noise of the world and come to Christ.

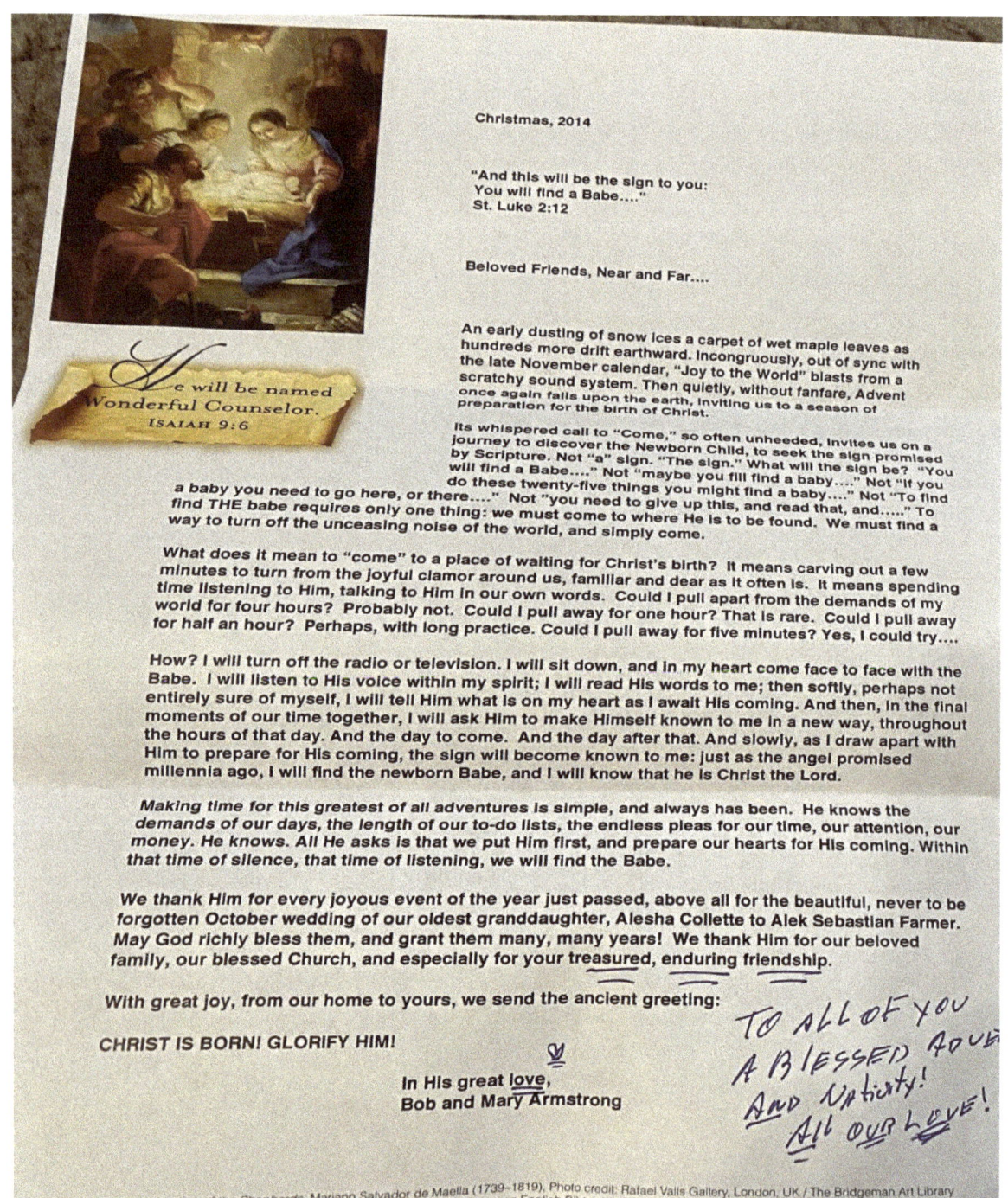

There is a section that is the theme of the Armstrongs' life. "He knows the demand of our days, the length of our to-do lists, the endless pleas for our time, our attention, our money . . . all he asks is that we put Him first and prepare our hearts for his coming. Within that time of silence, that time of listening, we will find the babe."

Though this letter is written for Christmas, it reflects how the Armstrongs kept their eyes on Christ through prayer so that they could be His presence to others.

Birthdays

YOU ARE SPECIAL

Whenever someone had a birthday, they had their cake and ice cream on a You are Special plate. I remember they were usually red with white writing. Somehow Mary's was broken.

She and Bob embraced frugality, and they often found what they needed that was like new and cost a fraction of the price at thrift stores. When something happened Mary would pray and wait. She had long ago learned how to listen to God.

She came back so excited from shopping one day and showed us what she found. It was a grayish-white stoneware "You are Special" plate with the writing in blue. It was a spectacular find. I asked how she found it. She said, "It was the Holy Spirit." Even in the small things God hears us.

The plate was a celebration of the person and of the image of God in whom they were made.

We are made in the image of God, and the goal of the Christian is to live in union with Christ and become more like him.

In doing this Bob and Mary celebrated the image of God in that person.

On this plate would be a luscious piece of frozen chocolate mint ice cream pie. It would come with a small thoughtful gift and usually a wonderful handmade card. For those who had the blessing of this experience you truly felt special and loved.

Below is a picture of Mary for the occasion of a summer birthday. If there was a birthday, there was ice cream.

Unknown source *Bob and Mary celebrating Bob*

Big Move—First House

1997 was a pivotal year for me. After two years of substitute teaching and applying to school districts, I was hired after a phone interview to teach first grade at Bendorf Elementary School in Las Vegas, Nevada.

I was thirty-four years old and excited for the first time to be a successful adult. I traveled to Las Vegas and stayed with my uncle. While there I leased an apartment and would stay there for five years. It was a nice upstairs unit and was about fifteen minutes from work.

Bob and Mary had prepared me well and prayed for me. Mary recalled how she made sure her sons knew how to prepare some basic foods when they went to college. One of those was quesadillas with guacamole. She sent two recipe cards along with a card and a lovely message that fed more than food.

...may it be among your very best.

Just a little something for our godson as you are involved in some of your new duties. We love you!!! You are awesome!

Happy, Happy Birthday beloved godson! May this reed giftie add new joy to your love of cooking! God grant you many, many, many years! We love you! THE GODPARENTS

Recipe for: QUESADILLAS

Ingredients:

12 (or more, depending on appetites!) 8" FLOUR tortillas

Slices of sharp cheddar-Jack cheese

1 can chopped chiles (mild or hot, depending on preference)

Cover one tortilla with thin slices of cheese. Top with a good sprinkling of well-drained chiles. Top with second tortilla. Thinly butter top of tortilla. Repeat assembling tortillas; stack on plate.

Bake (fry) tortillas on teflon or other hot griddle - about 350 - 400 degrees. Turn each tortilla when bottom is slightly browned; cook other side until cheese is almost melted. Cut tortillas into 4 pieces each & stack on plates or platter. Serve with guacamole!

Recipe for: GUACAMOLE

Ingredients:

Several ripe avocados
one large onion
Hot pepper or chile powder or cayenne pepper as desired
Chopped chiles, well drained, if desired

Mash several avocados with fork or food processor. Scrape juice from cut onion (several tablespoons - as desired) & mix into mashed avocados. Stir in hot pepper &/or chopped chiles, if desired.

Serve with quesadillas...& a green salad...ENJOY!

HINT: Use spoon to scrape juice from onion...
       taste as you go!

My fifth year teaching was 2001, and I had a choice to stay in Nevada or go back to Washington. It took a lot of hard work to get to this point in my life, and I was honestly afraid of taking chances now that I had tenure.

I had built a life in Nevada, and I was independent, had a little money in the bank, and when I thought of Washington, I remembered failure. I decided to buy a two-bedroom, two-bath condo and not pay for rent receipts but begin to acquire some equity.

It was a lovely purchase, and I lived there until I married Olga in 2014. Bob and Mary sent me a gift that I know took time to make. It is a beautiful Orthodox cross to hang in my home. It was symbolic of how far together with their prayers, I had come. The cross was the path of that journey. It was not easy; however, I am so grateful to God they were at my side with prayer and encouragement along the way. While I chose not to live in Washington, I would spend Christmas and summer with them.

Cross made by Bob to celebrate the purchase of my home.

Celebratory People

The Armstrongs were prayerful and fun people. Many were drawn to them because of their lively conversation, their sense of humor, and laughter. They loved people and loved having a good time. Most pictures you will see Bob and Mary smiling and laughing. Socializing energized them. As can be gleaned from previous stories it did not matter what background a person came from. They were loved and accepted.

The Christian Faith and the Orthodox Church were the center of Bob and Mary's life. They were active in each faith group they were a part of, and being involved in church and living it out in the world was part of their spiritual DNA.

The most fun we had together was at meals. The meals were only the place to meet. They could be at a friend's house, or a restaurant. I have no memory of this picture. Bob and Mary seem to get the joke. I look like I am sleeping through it.

Unknown Source   Mary Armstrong's photo

Then there is the picture that has no explanation, but we're having a good time. The banner in the background says happy birthday—for whom is unknown.

We appear to be holding cans of bug killer and smiling. I like to eliminate bugs as much as the next guy, just not that much that I would be holding a can of spray. We were easy to amuse.

John and Rita with Bob and Mary

Here is a lovely picture of John and Rita with Bob and Mary for John's birthday. The meal was just the setting for the good talk and fellowship. This picture represents the good time that anyone who shared a meal with Bob and Mary experienced.

Photo courtesy of John Goddard

This picture was taken not long before their repose at BoonDockers.
They are tired but still enjoyed good food and fellowship.

Hospitality

Bob and Mary loved to have people over their house. Bob and Mary had it down to a science of how to have a successful party. For an event to function well it must be well-planned and organized, and Bob and Mary did this supremely well. Everything for an outdoor party would be prepared in advance except for food. Containers for drinks would be set up ready for ice.

Tables covered, chairs out, and Mary preparing the final touches. As guests arrived, after light snacks and conversation, Bob would barbecue, Mary would prepare the final touches, and then the guests would gather for a great meal, a great time, with lots of conversation and laughter.

Bob Made Great BBQ

And Mary Made Great Salad

One of the things that Mary was known for was her delicious salads. They were rich in a variety of greens, avocados, fresh croutons, and peanuts. The salad was then topped with a delicious dressing that was fresh, zesty, crisp, and refreshing. Here is her salad dressing recipe. If you asked for the recipe, Mary would type it on a three-by-five card.

On the opposite side she tells how the salad could be a dinner salad. Mary always had a menu in mind, and when a side dish could become a main course or part of one, all the better.

She had an old typewriter in her office. In would go the 3-by-5 card and in minutes out would come the recipe card with directions on both sides. I have seldom seen someone type so well so fast.

She also loved all things chicken which is reflected in this card.

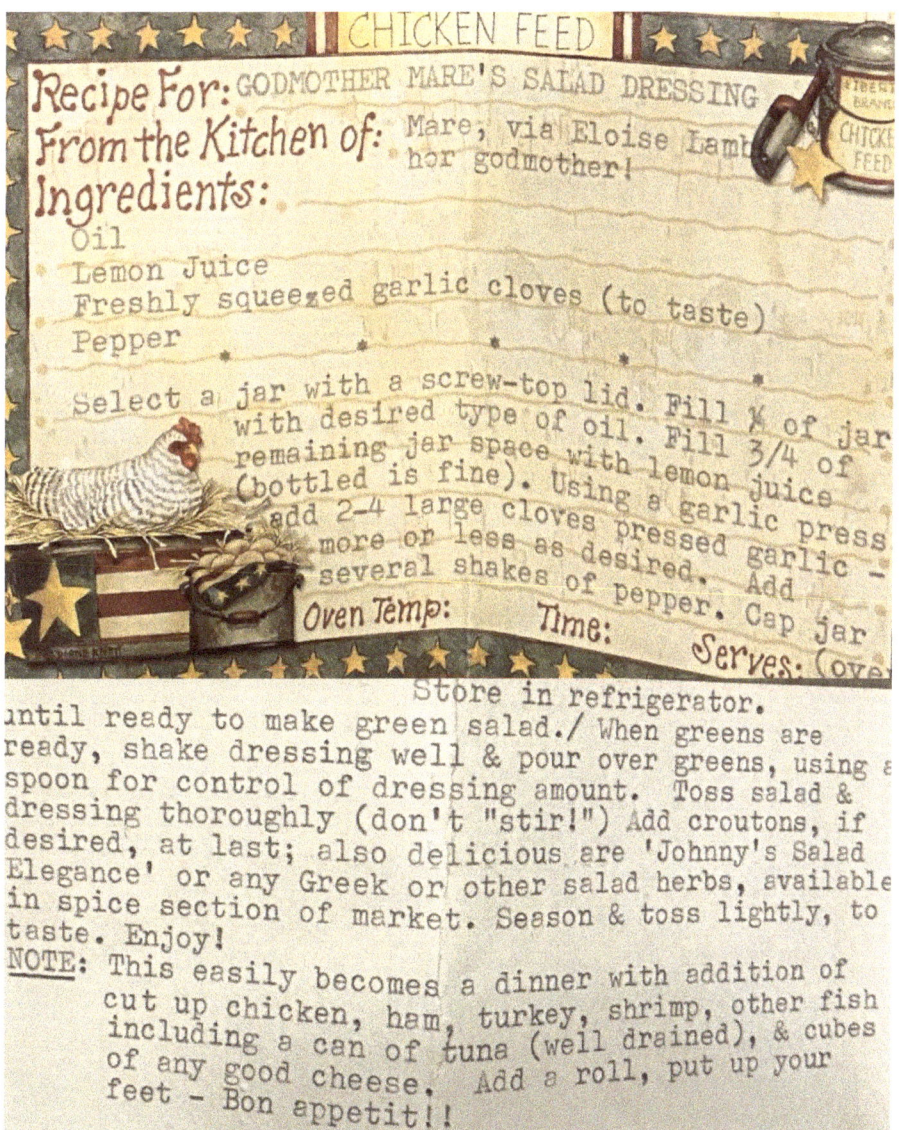

And everyone enjoyed it.

Becoming like the Light—Christlike

While most people would say they want to be like Bob and Mary, they would say better to be yourself with Christ. Bob would tell me frequently that God made only one Tony Willey, and while I heard with my ears, the darkness inside of me did not see the truth in what he said.

What I really wanted to be was what Bob modeled. A strong Christian man, with an inner core centered on Christ, who knew who he was, and to whom he belonged.

God molds each of us differently using the sun and shade of life to shape us. The grace of Bob and Mary was that they used those periods of sun and shade to follow Christ in both circumstances.

I knew Bob and Mary in the autumn of their lives. The hard work of life was mastered.

Both had broken marriages, and both would acknowledge these as failures. They mourned the loss of Chris and cared for an ailing and challenging mother-in-law.

They made themselves available to God's grace trusting Him in the sun, shade, and storms of lives.

To be that man that I want to be I must do the same and take up my cross and follow Christ in times of joy, sorrow, and everything in between.

Mary found "that the fruit of the spirit doesn't ripen after all the jobs are done, the fruit grows in the midst of the work, probably because of it." Mary, who was always very organized, learned to accept because she found that "Drudgery, interruptions, and confusion came from the outside . . . The Spirit works within, if only I give him a chance." **Ibid, p. 219**

Mary found we live it by listening to God and seeing him act amidst the challenges of our lives. She always loved to garden, and these experiences produced the beautiful fruits that continued to grow until she went to be with Him.

I must be open to seeing in every situation and person the hand of God. It may mean suffering and self-denial, but in trying to do so we become who we are meant to be in Christ by embracing His cross.

Watchful Heart and Mind

Bob and Mary's discipline of daily prayer, active church attendance, and participation in the life of the church focused their hearts to God and their hands to their neighbors.

In *Caregiving for Your Loved Ones*, Mary writes "that anger and its close cousin bitterness are the most common baggage for caregivers." I would go one step further and say it is the chief ailment of our culture today. Families may or may not have a faith component in their lives, nor may they have an ability to actively listen to each other. The mind in these conditions becomes an easy place for anger and bitterness to abide. The only antidote is, as Mary writes, daily vigilance. **Ibid p. 226**

> Fatigue, painful memories, and caregiving's never-ending demands often force open the window of bitterness. It slips in unseen, like damp night air through a crack. We don't realize it's there until we're shivering.
>
> The sole antidote is daily vigilance. Over and over, we need to lock the window of our soul against a bitter spirit. Like bees in the garden, we must fly to the warmth and light of Christ's forgiving presence. Only He can evaporate the chill and remove our dark resentment.
>
> But bitterness never disappears forever. It retreats to lick its wounds, still searching for unguarded windows. Sooner or later, on the cold winds of harsh words, a sharp tongue, or lingering guilt, it will creep in once more. We must daily be on guard, lest bitterness set up housekeeping in our souls.
>
> **PRAYER:** I feel so weak, Father, and sometimes so far from You. Warm me, Lord, and keep me sweet. In Jesus' name. Amen.

See to it . . . that no root of bitterness springing up causes trouble (Hebrews 12:12-15).

This section applies not just to caregiving but to all in daily life. Living today is fast-paced and we are bombarded with expectations from family, employers, and ourselves. Fatigue sets in, and with it the mind begins to be frustrated at not being able to respond to the stimuli.

This frustration leads to anger, and long term, to resentment that can be associated with a spouse, child, mother, or anyone who is the "cause" of the resentment.

Then comes bitterness and once established is hard to root out. The only way to make it shrink away is to focus the light of Christ on it. This requires watchfulness and a willingness to admit one has it and then to work at its removal through prayer and the help of clergy. Bitterness is an evil beast because, as Mary writes, it hides and attacks when unguarded.

That is why a watchful heart is so necessary. A watchful heart is a humble and honest heart that admits its pain to God and repents of it and asks for God's grace to change.

Bob and Mary never became bitter because they trusted in the love of God. They grieved, they mourned, they cried, they experienced grief but kept it healthy because they knew how toxic it was for all that they loved.

Matthew

Matthew was the little boy who sat with his mother looking at a flower. He was the young man who went to Marine Boot Camp with his family celebrating and showing their love and the sweetness of his mom's German chocolate cake in his mouth.

While he was not given length of years, what he accomplished with those thirty-five years is truly remarkable.

Matt received a fine education, and he parlayed it into obtaining a position at Smith Kline Beecham, which is one of the largest pharmaceutical companies in the world. In his position as a Senior Pharmaceutical Consultant, he advised companies on the pharmaceutical products developed by the company.

He was a beloved husband, father, son, brother, and uncle. When he passed, the fabric of the family was torn.

"The truly Orthodox person always has both feet firmly on the ground, facing whatever situation is right in front of him. It is in accepting given situations, which requires a loving heart, that one encounters God."
Seraphim Rose God's Revelation to the Human Heart, p. 25

Bob, Mary, and their family had this in the full as they took care of Matt.

The goal of this book is to hear and see Bob and Mary; the best way is to read their own words. Mary sent me a beautiful letter recalling the last five days of Matthew's life. She writes from a mother's heart of their shared experience. It is a remarkable document and speaks well of the entire family, their love for God, as demonstrated in their care of Matthew.

There is nothing that I can add or expand on. The letter states better than I could the entire family's faith, love, and care for Matt as well as Bob and Mary's deeply lived Orthodox faith.

> The Lord is my shepherd; I shall not want. PSALM 23:1

21 July, 1999
Prophet Ezekiel

Hi, Beloved Godson,

How we have felt your love and prayers during the past difficult months and weeks! You have surrounded us with such caring, through phone calls, BEAUTIFUL cards, and most generous gifts. THANK YOU, beloved Tony...we shall always thank God for His gift of you.

Your letter accompanying your card of sympathy touched us deeply - yes, you could indeed say he was beautiful! Your words, theme of the letter, and deep caring meant so much - we shall treasure it for years to come.

May God richly, enduringly bless you for your most generous, thoughtful gift for the boys' scholarship fund! We have passed it on to Rita, who is "doing the math"....Lori will learn of all donors, but NOT amounts. She of course already is aware of your kindness, and is so very grateful.

And for my Starbucks (well, OUR!!) gift....after the vicelike grip of the past weeks, Bob and I look forward hugely to a coffee/tea/brioche break, with time just for each other, time to look back...and ahead...with our Lord. We shall clink coffee/tea mugs as we sit there, and thank God, again, for you!

-two-

We were so sorry to miss your call on July 3....we'd gone on down to Vespers, not knowing that Matt's final crisis would begin in days. All the same, it was a very happy thing to arrive later, and hear your voice. And speaking of your voice, let's turn to your feet...is this perchance your sock? We've meant to send it for ages...the other one may be long gone by now!

The final five days of Matt's life were a struggle, but an incredible privilege for the many family members who literally lived at Matt and Lori's house during that time. John pulled his motor home into the cul-de-sac, hooked up to power and water with a neighbor's blessing, and stayed for the duration. Lori's parents took over the kitchen: great meals, pots of coffee, nibblers for everyone. Bob and Matt's friend Scott literally washed, folded, and put away dozens of loads of wash...and helped turn and lift Matt when we needed muscles. Rita, as always, took over the children and watering the pots outside...she never stopped. My sister Mimi, Lori, and I nursed Matt around the clock, overseen by Hospice...he truly lacked for nothing.

We have NEVER been more grateful for the Orthodox faith: we had candles burning in front of a travel icon of the Lord and His Holy Mother, 24 hours a day. We had prayers many times from the Prayer Books, and continued to anoint Matt with oil and tears from the Weeping Icon in Blanco, Texas. I prayed Evening Prayers, holding Matt's hand, the night before his death, and Morning Prayers just hours before he died. Thank God for the ancient, holy prayers of the Church! When we see you we will share more details...suffice it

-three-

to say it was totally a home death, with all the family - even the dog, Lucy - gathered around his bed. All glory and praise to God!

We enclose a program of the funeral, which about 250 people attended, and a copy of the obituary. The funeral was beautiful- Matt wasn't Catholic, but was perhaps headed that way - Fr. Horatio (priest from the Philippines) was tender, eloquent, and totally loving. Lori stood at the back of the Church, personally thanking each person who came! I sat up in front, escorted by the Very Rev. A. James Bernstein, and I have NEVER been more thankful in my life- his presence was an incredible help and encouragement. Bob was a pallbearer, and though with me for the actual service, had to be otherwise occupied the rest of the time.

We are gradually regaining physical strength, returning to the holy and most blessed gift of the daily routine, and have a beautiful icon of St. Matthew, flowers, other icons, and candle burning whenever we are home, in our little den. We shall keep it there until August 18, the end of the Forty Day Prayers. Many are remembering Matt through this time, using the Prayers for the Dead in the red or blue Prayer Books, and we know you will join us in this vigil.

God bless and keep you, and grant you great joy in your life and work. We shall never forget your love and kindness during this most fiery trial we have endured...

We love you dearly, in Him,

Bob and Mary

After Bob's birthday in July, I received a letter from Bob. Again, I am going to let the letter speak for itself. He reflects on how he and Mary are doing and the impact of Matthew's repose.

> Dear Tony,
>
> Whew! Mary and I are slowly recovering from the last five months — from Matt's first CAT scan to his death. Things are looking up and with the Lord's help and the prayers of our church family and friends and family we will come out the other side of this very great sadness our Lord has permitted us to experience. It will be quite some time until we grasp the full import of this event.
>
> Thank you so for my Birthday Gift, a Hardware Store is calling me! And for your gift to the Goddard Boys Education Fund.
>
> -2-
>
> It is already many thousands of dollars.
>
> You can rest assured you will be with us in spirit as we enter Starbucks to enjoy your gift! Very thoughtful, too.
>
> Rich Spiler's Father died last week in Port Townsend. The service will be in a couple of weeks, probably in the Port Angeles area. I will send you more information when it is available.
>
> Thank you also for your thoughtful and generous gifts! We hope you will come back to the Puget Sound area before this year is out.
>
> God Bless you,
> Bob

As Mary wrote in an email, "if it were not for the church, its peace, beauty, closeness to our Lord, EVERYTHING—I would have drowned in a sea of grief years ago. It's a total solace and joy—I feel the Lord's presence wash over me like waves every time I walk in."

Matthew and Lori's son, Tony, passed away suddenly on November 30, 2011. He was mourned by all who knew and loved him. The loss of their grandson was a severe blow to Bob and Mary and the entire family. Bob and Mary's deep faith sustained them as it did in their previous times of mourning.

Though their grief was intense, they found their way through to the other side, to the light of Christ. They prayed for their much loved son and grandson's eternal rest and peace to the end of their days.

Courtesy Jacob McGinnis
Arm in Arm helping the other in their walk with God.

Light of Contentment

Godliness with contentment is a great gain. Bob and Mary were retired, and though their income was limited, their standard of living was not. They created a wealth of beauty in their home, church, and neighborhood. When you entered their home, everything was a combination of their two lives becoming one.

They did not need the newest appliances, and did not have a cell phone until just before passing. Mary's computer was refurbished and Bob steadfastly kept his distance from it. Their cars were all second- or third-hand. Everything they owned was well-maintained.

They drew upon their experience of growing up during the Great Depression of the 1930s and World War II by being frugal. They were not bound by things.

Their real joy came in their family, their church, and inviting people to their home in Fair Havens.

Their raised garden allowed them to pursue their love for gardening while supplying them with fresh vegetables and fruit. Nearby blackberry bushes provided fresh delicious fruit in the summer, which was gathered and served in winter with vanilla ice cream.

They cut coupons, and when Mary did the weekly shopping, she would go to three stores to get the best buys. She did not go randomly but with a menu in mind so that she would have exactly what she needed to prepare home-cooked meals. Any leftovers would go in the fridge or freezer.

Bob found a way to add income by making an apartment from a portion of the garage to rent. It was a small, clean, modern unit that was never empty and provided a much-needed additional income.

Their values of faith, hope, love of God and others and habits of frugality allowed them to live a life of real value whose worth rested in the love of God and neighbor.

Cherishing the Moments

I remember when Mary's health started to fail and going to medical appointments began to take more time out of their day. The appointments were at the main Providence Hospital, which is near Puget Sound.

Bob and Mary before leaving would pack a lunch and then go to her appointment. Instead of going directly home they would go near the water or other pretty locations and have a nice picnic before going home. Together they would chat about the appointment, pray, and enjoy being together in the moment.

Creating Community

This deep faith in God and love for their neighbor was tangible to nearly all who met them. Mary brought cookies to the bank teller. Their neighborhood was a miniature village. The neighbors spoke to each other and liked each other, not just one but all of them.

I loved to take Bob and Mary to BoonDockers. The owners were Muslim and loved them. They shared a commonality of having veterans in the family. They would often come and chat. I had lunch with them, and they still remember them with fondness.

Another activity was the Friday Club that met at McDonalds. It consisted of the loveliest bunch of senior citizens one could imagine.

Together they exchanged jokes, shared stories, and enjoyed each other's company while enjoying their coffee.

If we were in a fasting period, we would be feasting on fries, and those not fasting would be enjoying breakfast sandwiches with meat. These gatherings were a delight, and it was a joy to hang out with the coolest couple in the world.

As I reflect on my life after Bob and Mary, I realize the impact they have had on life and my marriage. Bob looked at every moment as an opportunity to serve. It could be small, like getting Mary a cup of coffee, or going to the local print shop and having something printed for Mary's scrapbook project, or mailing something in the afternoon. It was not received as an inconvenience or burden but an opportunity to love her and in doing it he loved her more and she, him.

Bob and Mary's numerous acts of kindness, generosity, and prayer have enabled me to see these unexpected moments as opportunities of grace. They may not be desired, and can be painful; however, they do and can bring one closer to God through loving one's neighbor.

Do Everything in Jesus Christ

The more our minds and hearts are in union with Christ, the more our daily actions in life will reflect this and we will be Christophers, Christ-Bearers in the world.

Bob and Mary were the same godly people they were in their homes as they were when in the community. They began their journey of faith as Episcopalians and completed it as Orthodox Christians.

At each point in their faith journeys Christ was present. The fullness of their faith was completed in the Orthodox Church. They carried within them the light of Christ, which illumined their whole life, and all those who were blessed to know them.

Christ lived in them, and they shared the fruit of the Holy Spirit with all who knew them and met them.

Nothing in their lives was mundane; every act can be a blessed and spiritual act of love to God. Going to the bank and bringing cookies, knowing everyone's name at the Marysville co-op, going to the doctors, paying the bills, writing emails, sending godchildren cards, teaching Sunday school, being the bathroom monitor. All their lives and actions were aimed to bring the love of Christ by word and deed.

The work of God is to love him, and believe in the one He sent. We all saw this in the Armstrongs. They lived their lives intentionally focused on Christ. While I will never be Bob, Bum, or John, I can be who Christ means me to be and live a life orienting myself to Him by resisting that which gets in the way of union with Him, such as ego, sin, and selfishness. As I do that, I can be Him in my daily life and do those small works of mercy to the people God gives me in the moment.

This gives freedom from the fears of the world and what the media sells. Bob and Mary followed Christ and led a rich, joyful inner and outer life. They were not boring, sour, or mundane, they were engaging and a joy to all who knew them. That is the goal of my life.

The Ladder of Virtues

II Peter 1:5-7
II Peter 1:5-7 is a ladder of acquiring step-by-step the virtues needed in living a godly life in Christ.

It is a perfect description of how they lived their lives in Christ, and with others.

Add to your faith virtue, to your virtue knowledge, to knowledge self-control, to self-control perseverance, to perseverance godliness, to godliness brotherly kindness and to brotherly kindness love.

Bob and Mary lived this ladder of faith. Their lives were dedicated to the communities of faith that they belonged to. Their virtues of kindness, faithfulness, and love for all only grew with time.

To this they added knowledge. Bob and Mary were high church Episcopalians and as that church changed, they found they could not stay. They discovered the Orthodox Church. Their faith grew in depth as they lived the fullness of the faith.

To knowledge self-control. Bob and Mary had strong personalities. They learned to master their passions, those things in all of us whether it is anger or a sharp wit, and turn it into something positive. Perseverance—they never quit.

They both lost a marriage; Mary lost two sons and a grandson. She had cancer, and Bob suffered seeing her in pain. They mourned, they hurt, but they pressed on. This perseverance created godliness in faith and action that continued until they reposed.

Last, brotherly kindness and love. This is the fruit of the ladder of these virtues. Kindness is the expression of love, and love when it is lived provides warmth in a cold and dark world because it prepares the heart for the love of God.

The fruit of prayer led them to find those moments for acts of kindness. Kindness creates warm hearts and healthy relationships, and Bob and Mary were instruments of that kindness.

II Peter 1:8 describes the result of living these virtues. "For if these things are yours and they abound, you will neither be barren nor unfruitful in the knowledge of our Lord Jesus Christ." Bob and Mary lived fruitful and grace-filled lives in Christ, and the good fruits of that life were abundant and clear for all to see.

Nearing the Top of the Ladder

Toward the Light
Mary's Voice
Every writer has a voice, you could hear her voice in everything she wrote, especially in her emails. It is in those emails seven years after her passing that I can sense her presence.

> **Sat, Aug 22, 2015 at 3:48 PM**
>
> **Hi Toners!**
>
> **WONDERFUL email...we'll take it going ahead or going backwards!**
>
> **Your classroom is a wonder....any kid walking into it would be in ecstasy - AWESOME JOB!**

> Mimi sent us the Facebook picture of you & Olga, so we knew of your getaway.....CONGRATULATIONS ON TWO YEARS!!! The celebration sounds like a total class act, even if the Trump Hotel was a bit over the top....like Mr. Trump himself!
>
> Love, love the pictures....truly worth a thousand words....most of all the one of our beloved godson serving at the altar! You are so involved in so many lives...may God continue to use you to His glory!
>
> All is well here - we're feeling very virtuous because today we defrosted the huge garage freezer, which had gone TWO years....too long.....lots of ice buildup. It's all shipshape now, all ice gone, neat as a pin. Whew!
>
> Highpoint of past several months was our Metropolitan Joseph's visit to our area - he visited every local church, then came to St. Paul last Sunday for a Hierarchical Liturgy & to ordain our beloved Sbdn. Jeremiah Vollman to the Diaconate. A total joy to see His Eminence, AND the ordination!
>
> I'm now 7 weeks out from end of chemo, & feeling stronger every day. SO aware of holy St. George with me every minute - your beautiful medal is an ongoing gift.
>
> Huge hugs to Olga & any guys who are there - you run a revolving door!
>
> We love you!!
>
> The GPs
> P.S. Watch the mailbox...a certain package will land there soon! :)

This is a special email. Mary had fought cancer for a couple of years. When I was home that summer, she had lost her hair due to chemo and was wearing a cap. The amazing thing was, through all the chemo, she was still Mary.

In this email she calls me Toners, which was the name that Bob and Mary called me, and I treasure it. Then there is the enjoyment of the pictures and the compliment of me reading the Epistle.

She and Bob were preparing so that if Mary did repose, he would have a clean freezer full of food. There was the joy she had in our church seeing the Metropolitan Ordain Father Jeremiah Vollman to the Diaconate.

Finally, there was, "I'm now 7 weeks out from end of chemo, & feeling stronger every day."

Looking back, that really hurt because it was a phantom remission. Her hair had barely begun to grow back.

Going to the Light

I believed that she would win this fight despite the evidence. Denial creates its own reality. They had been with us so long that I thought and wished it would be longer.

We were in the den, and she was on the couch reclining, and I asked her what happens if your treatments do not work. She said then I go to my Savior who I have loved with all my heart, all my life.
They made sure that each was aware of where the important documents were and how to turn on the computer.

When I returned to Nevada, Mary was still strong. Going into the fall she declined, lost weight, and weakened to the point that Hospice Services were needed.

I did not go at that point to see her because this was the family's time to say goodbye. However, I was given the gift of saying goodbye by phone. By that time Mary could barely talk. I told her I loved her and to pray for me when she reached Heaven. She said she would. She reposed the next day, November 22, 2015.

Resting in the Light

Her funeral was beautiful. The prayers the congregation said together was a plea and an act of faith. A plea to God to take care of this dear lady who so many loved and an act of faith that He would. It rained during the burial.

The finality of life and the finality of death was driven home by the thump of dirt upon the casket's wooden top. I looked at the grave at the muddy sides and realized you cannot take anything with you and was happy that Mary had chosen love, compassion, care, faith, and humility over material things. She and Bob were immeasurably richer because of their choices.

After Mary

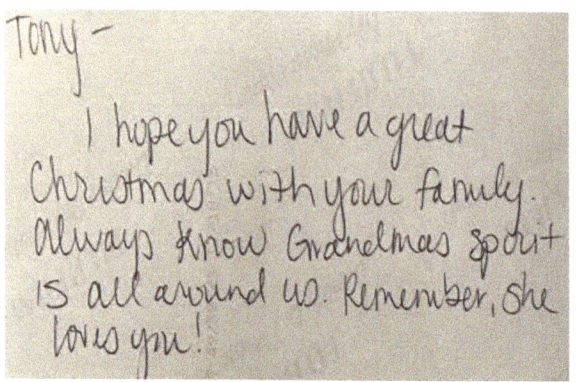

Bob spent November and December celebrating Thanksgiving and Christmas with John, Rita, and family. John and Rita's eldest daughter sent me a Christmas card with this inscription.

Mary's spirit was with us in the thoughtfulness and kindness of her family. This card touched me then and now because it is like the dream where Mary laughed at death, and here she is saying she loves me.

Bob continued with his blessed "rut of routine." Family and friends stopped by and called. The house was empty of the one he loved best. It was too quiet without her presence.

Church was a must for Bob. It was home; here were people he watched grow up and was a godfather and mentor to numerous others. Here were familiar faces and voices. Here was his second home, and he could sit in the same place that he sat in with Mary. He knew he was loved but age and loss were sapping his strength.

The loss of Mary was devastating to Bob. It was a tough blow at age eighty-seven to recover from. Most of us hoped he would be with us for another year. I talked to Bob a couple of times on the phone.

In this photo Bob is helped by godson
Courtesy of Muehleisen Family

John after receiving communion.

His mind slipped back in time, and he thought I was someone else. I was concerned and called John and found that indeed Bob was slipping cognitively. It did not happen often, but he was eighty-seven, and it was not unexpected.

Bob was healthy except for his lungs. He had bouts of pneumonia previously that had damaged them. He used a C-pap machine for sleep apnea. These machines needed to be cleaned daily. If they are not cleaned germs and bacteria grow and then the unit becomes hazardous to the patient.

While Mary was alive, she kept it clean. After her passing, this fell to Bob. Bob had just lost his wife. He was alone in the house, and he was emotionally lost without Mary. He may have attempted to clean it, and he may have forgotten for several days. By late December he was ill with pneumonia again.

Amazingly, as he was going through all this, he sent me a lovely Christmas card.

All these years later it still makes me emotional to read this. He has lost his wife, his health is declining, and he took the time and expended the energy to send a beautiful card and a Starbucks card. He wanted to remind me to create lines of communication, and to follow Mary's advice that we take time for each other like they did with a trip out of the house for coffee together.

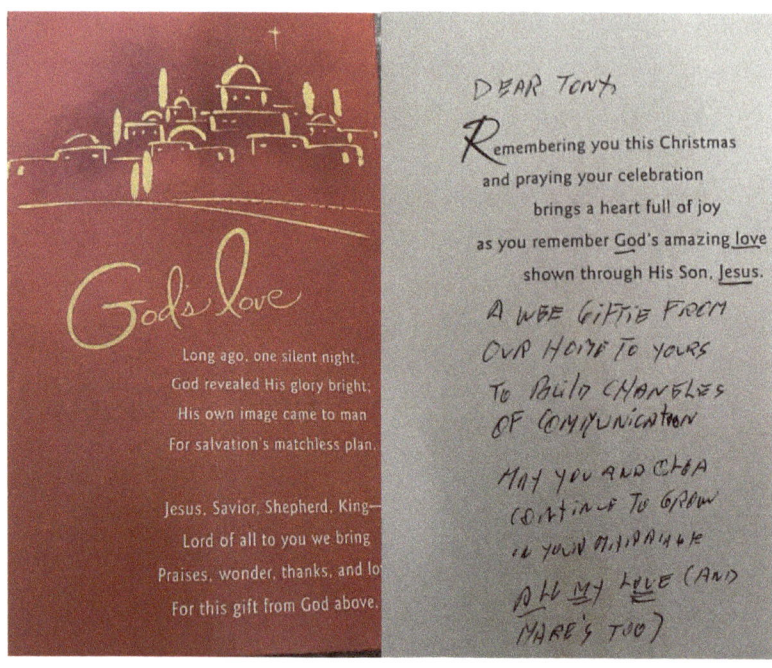

Bob signed for both, himself and Mary. She may have been in Heaven already, but she was always present in his heart.

This was Bob always kind, loving, living his faith. He was not showy, but he was real, and that brought stability to us all. The card prepared me for his call in January. I knew he was not feeling well, and I was not surprised when He said I needed to let him go, that he loved me, and I was his brother in Christ.

He called me from the hospital. I was in church. It was just after old calendar Christmas. I don't remember exactly what I said. I think it was "Go to Mary." He said I was his brother in Christ. I told him I loved him. In my heart, I knew he wanted to be with Mary. It was the last time we talked. I was grateful I could say goodbye to the only "real" father I have known and the gift of God that saved my life.

He passed on January 16, 2016. A parishioner Bob invited to lunch each week was with him at the hospital and said that when Bob passed, he saw him get up out of bed and go toward an opening that appeared in the room. In the opening he saw light, and Bob walked into it. I am sure one of the first persons he met was Mary.

I flew to Washington the next day, arriving at night. It was dark, and I was in a rental car. Brier and Lynwood are a maze and my sense of direction poor, especially at night. After wandering around lost for half an hour, I said to Bob, in prayer, "If you want me to get to church, you're going to have to help me get there." Ten minutes later I was there.

I remember missing the fact that I did not hold his hand as he passed. It did not make sense, but it was a fact. In looking at the picture of him with his father, the two hands touching, I think I understand why I felt that way. I wanted to touch the hands of the man who had been my father in all the ways that mattered most. I went inside and found him in his casket.

He was beautiful. I grasped his hand. It was warm and flexible, and I held it for a few minutes. I knew he was in the hands of God and that wound was now healed by the Father who wipes every eye and heals all wounds that loved and never abandoned him and was now with Him forever.

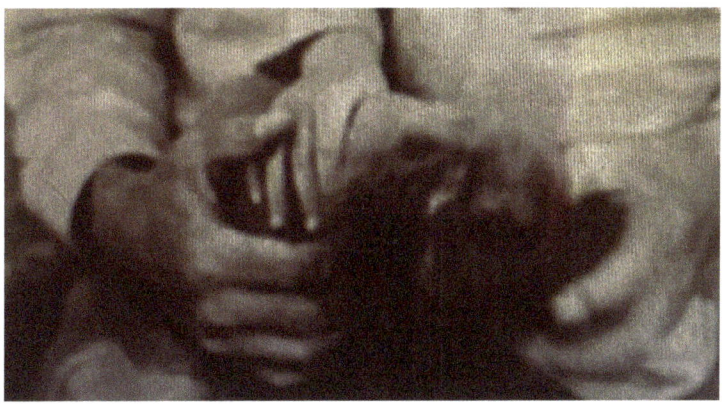

Looking upon him was like viewing a Viking King; all he needed was his long sword. It would be appropriate. In life he wielded the sword of the Spirit and scripture, which is the word of God, which he knew so well to defeat the darkness of sin.

His funeral was quiet, serene, and peaceful, as he was. What I remember most is being asked last minute to be a pallbearer. It was totally unexpected. We walked him from the hearse to the grave. Bob and I went for many walks, and this last was a moment of perfect symmetry and grace; we walked during our pilgrimage together, we walked together to his earthly rest.

Flowers were thrown in the grave along with the now all-too-familiar sound of dirt hitting the wooden coffin. It was and is still painful to remember these twin losses that happened so close together. It is beautiful to know though that they are both with God, their hearts' true home.

Father James expressed with deep sorrow what we all felt at Bob's funeral: "What will we do without you?" The loss of Bob and Mary left a large chasm in all our hearts.

We did what Bob and Mary so often did. We wept, we mourned, we remembered, we prayed, and we trusted in the love of Christ and His providence. We know we will see them again, only next time we would see them in the reflection of God's glory and their true selves. We then continued our lives of faith as they did when they experienced loss and as they expected us to do as well.

Bob and Mary were known and loved by the congregations of Saint Paul, Saint Andrew, and Saint Thomas. They had numerous godchildren. The Holy Spirit comforted us, and gradually we overcame our grief. We warmed ourselves with their memory and our faith in God.

Light Overcomes Darkness

I had a dream about Mary one night. She was sitting in the den with her comfortable clothes, and I was with her. It felt great to be with her. She looked healthy and vibrant. Then I remembered that she was dead. I said, "Mary, didn't you die?" and she just laughed. With faith and love, they drew near to Christ in life and in their repose. Death was overcome, and both are alive in Christ.

Legacy of the Light

If Bob and Mary were to miraculously walk through the door of Saint Paul's unseen, they would see that what they started as founding parishioners is thriving. The church is active, has abundant young people, an active Sunday school, and bookstore. Father Jeremiah, who Bob and Mary saw come into the church as a catechumen, is the loving priest and father of a vital and active congregation.

They would not recognize all the people, but that would not stop them from getting to know them. Men and women are still entering the church, and I know that they would be added to their prayer list. Men and women are falling in love, babies born and baptized, and Mary would be making something special for all, with her ever-busy hands.

If they could sit unseen by their family, they would be full of joy. Matt and Laurie's sons are happy and leading productive and fulfilling lives. John and Rita's daughters are all married, with children of their own. The siblings and their spouses are close, and the family unit is tight.

Striving to Live the Light—My Life Now

I am immensely blessed. Thanks to the twenty years that Bob and Mary loved and prayed for me I continue to grow into the man that I am meant to be, by grace rather than circumstance.

I choose to no longer live my life confined in that box crafted by Robert W. when he shot me with cigarette butts. My confidence is based on the warmth and love of God, who is the light and life and my salvation.

Bob and Mary were truly the parents of my new life. Mary said that I would change as I took part in the sacrament of communion. She was right.

The Miracle of a Sound Mind

The gift of a sound mind takes time and it did not come suddenly. The anxiety and fear resonated within me for a long time from invasive thoughts spawned by these evil twin monsters. They would enter my mind unbidden and uninvited. Once in they would they would repeat their ugly songs over and over again. While counciling mitigated their noise and intrusion, it did not remove it completely. This took years to happen, and if it were not for the Orthodox Church and Bob and Mary, I would still be haunted and distracted by them.

The cure came in the form of the Holy Sacraments of the church, particularly Holy Communion, along with the reading of scripture and books by and about the saints. As I read the lives of the saints, their courage and the strength of their faith inspired me to overcome my fear and increase my faith. I learned that faith in Christ banishes the evil twins, and the invasive thoughts slowly receded into the abyss.

Another avenue of grace was the prayer rope. It gave me a way to focus on the name of Christ and to ignore the thoughts. I gained step by step a renewed and freed mind.

This was not a smooth course. It was a struggle. I had to learn to let go of the thoughts and to hang onto Christ. It was also one that I know I could not have done alone. Only with the love of Christ, Bob and Mary, and the church was I able to gain a renewed mind. Which prepared me for the miracle of my life.

Recent Picture

When I was fifty, Bob and Mary's prayers, my partaking the sacraments, and God's grace led to a miracle. I was praying at home, and I felt the overwhelming love of God. My eyes were locked on the cross and waves of love washed over me.

The Orthodox Prayer to the Holy Cross describes well what happened to me. The enemies of my soul, the demons and fear that haunted my mind for so many years, were made to flee.

Orthodox Prayer to the Holy Cross (Let God Arise)
Let God arise, and let His enemies be scattered; and let those who hate Him flee from His face. As smoke vanishes, let them vanish; and as wax melts from the presence of fire, so let the demons perish from the presence of those who love God and who sign themselves with the Sign of the Cross and say with gladness: Hail, most precious and life-giving Cross of the Lord, for Thou drives away the demons by the power of our Lord Jesus Christ Who was crucified on thee, went down to hell and trampled on the power of the devil, and gave us thee, His honorable Cross, for driving away all enemies. O most precious and life-giving Cross of the Lord, help me with our holy Lady, the Virgin Theotokos, and with all the Saints throughout the ages. Amen.

What was lacking was given, that which was bent by circumstance and sin straightened. I was given a sound mind, free of all that encumbered it, and was healed.

I am always in awe when I recall this. The circumstances of my birth, childhood, no longer had power over me. Those shadows were dispersed by the warm love of God that washed over me. It was the love that I had been searching for all my life. I now had Christ as the center of my being.

I realized that I was a man and a Christian and no longer living in a defensive posture and afraid of life and the risks of living. In fact, a few months after the healing, I fell in love.

Bob and Mary would repose two years later. I think of this as a gift of God to ensure my continued growth in Christ. It was assurance to the Armstrongs and myself that I would continue to grow in faith and love after they reposed.

Thoughts and Fear of all the Years

I was made whole, but the devil still attempts to destroy our peace and souls by setting snares to trap us. Most of those are found in one's own mind. I was healed, but it did not mean that life was without temptation and challenges.

Saint Nectarios of Aegina captures perfectly our internal struggle:
We have within us deeply rooted weaknesses, passions, and defects. This cannot all be cut out with one sharp motion, but patience, persistence, care, and attention. The path leading to perfection is long.
https://www.orthodoxchurchquotes.com/2013/07/25/st-nectarios-of-aegina-we-have-within-us-deeply-rooted-weaknesses-passions-and-defects/

The mind has potential to be a vast storage house of fears, anger, and other passions, and these are what the devil uses to distract and attack us from the love of Christ and living our lives in Him. Like all men, I am subject to this. The devil attacks where a person is most vulnerable.

My weak point among others is fear of loss of people I love. It is rooted in my childhood and still rears its ugly head at unexpected times. It could be physical or relational.

In order to not get caught up in it I must ask myself if this perception is real. Almost 100 percent of the time it is not. The next thing I do is pray and, like Bob and Mary, trust God for a solution. The key for me is to not act on that perception; rather, I need to ask myself is this a real perception or one tainted by my past.

What I must not do is to put upon that person my unreasonable perceptions and judgments, my ideas of who that person is or how that person should be and do based on nothing more than my limited perceptions that are not based on reality.

If this occurs, then I no longer see the person as he or she is but an idol of my own creation with the power of a false god. This is blatant sin. It is creating an idol out of a person fleshed with my fears, judgments, and false expectations. It is idol worship, and it is completely unreal.

More importantly it is denying the image of God in that person and not loving my brother and sister and honoring God by loving who that person truly is.

C. S. Lewis in the following quote gives us a glimpse of who we are potentially in Christ. In this paragraph he gives a picture that makes me pause before ever judging or reducing a person into our image rather than God's.

"It is a serious thing to live in a society of possible gods and goddesses, to remember that the dullest most uninteresting person you can talk to may one day be a creature which, if you saw it now, you would be strongly tempted to worship, or else a horror and a corruption such as you now meet, if at all, only in a nightmare."

All day long we are, in some degree, helping each other to one or the other of these destinations. It is in the light of these overwhelming possibilities, it is with the awe and the circumspection proper to them, that we should conduct all of our dealings with one another, all friendships, all loves, all play, all politics. There are no ordinary people. You have never talked to a mere mortal. Nations, cultures, arts, civilizations—these are mortal, and their life is to ours as the life of a gnat. But it is immortals whom we joke with, work with, marry, snub, and exploit—immortal horrors or everlasting splendors." C.S. Lewis, <u>The Weight of Glory</u>, **Preached originally as a sermon in the church of Saint Mary the Virgin, Oxford, June 8 1942**

Thanks to the miracle, I can now discern reality versus the unreality that the devil may toss into my mind. However, I still have potential to fall and often do.

Saint Nectarios continues with encouraging words:
Patiently accept your falls and having stood up, immediately run to God, not remaining in that place where you have fallen.
https://www.orthodoxchurchquotes.com/2013/07/25/st-nectarios-of-aegina-we-have-within-us-deeply-rooted-weaknesses-passions-and-defects/

In other words, I need to stop what I am doing and run to God.
Do not despair if you keep falling into your old sins. Many of them are strong because they have the force of habit.
https://www.orthodoxchurchquotes.com/2013/07/25/st-nectarios-of-aegina-we-have-within-us-deeply-rooted-weaknesses-passions-and-defects/

That's the truth. When I was young, I lacked power, so I made myself feel powerful through fantasy. I did this for years and it indeed acquired the force of habit. It was an automatic response to the insecurity of relationships that snaps me back to this behavior. The encouragement is to never give into despair but to continue in faith.

Then I need to follow the very practical steps suggested by **Romans 12:18: If possible, so far as it depends on you, be at peace with all men.** What depends on me is to stay and communicate with the person I may have offended.

A beautiful example of this is when Bob said I was slothful. He apologized to me. He was right, but the relationship was more important than being right. He did it with humility and love and showed me a healthy way to be at peace with all men. When I am wrong, I need to be willing and try to mend that relationship.

Only with the passage of time and with fervor will they be conquered.

The life of a Christian is a marathon and not a sprint. By the time I knew Bob and Mary they had undergone trials of fire and were finely tuned instruments of God.

As I run my marathon, I can expect trials; however, with faith, fervor, persistence, and practicality, they can be overcome.

Don't let anyone deprive you of hope.

The following quote answers why hope is so important.

Hope is the assurance of the good outcome of our lives lived by faith in God. Hope is the power of certain conviction that the life built on faith will produce its fruits. Orthodox Church in America, Volume 4 Spirituality Orthodox Church in America
https://www.orthodoxchurchquotes.com/2013/07/25/st-nectarios-of-aegina-we-have-within-us-deeply-rooted-weaknesses-passions-and-defects/

Hope is the foundation of my faith in God and the key to persistent faith that no matter what, sin will be overcome, and our lives will bear fruit. Just like Bob and Mary.

Clean Cup and Platter and Our Offering to God

Luke 11:39-41
39 And the Lord said unto him, Now do you Pharisees make clean the outside of the cup and the platter; but your inward part is full of extortion and wickedness.

40 You fools, did not he that made that which is outside make that which is within also?

41 But rather give alms of such things as you have; and behold, all things are clean unto you.

Jesus is invited to eat with the Pharisees. Unlike them the Lord did not worry about cleaning the outside of the cup and platter. When the host pointed this out, The Lord responded with an astringent truth.

Now do you Pharisees make clean the outside of the cup and the platter; but your inward part is full of extortion and wickedness.

Christ is not talking about a cup or platter but the Pharisee and me. Sometime a truth is given gently and sometime pointedly so that it can be heard.

When the devil hits me and I fall and fail the Lord, I am full of wickedness. Like the Pharisee I need to act to get clean.

He shows a way out of wickedness to be clean.

41 But rather give alms of such things as you have; and behold, all things are clean unto you.

Give alms **such as you have**. We Christians are rich in spiritual gifts.

But the fruit of the Spirit is love, joy, peace, patience, kindness, goodness, faithfulness, gentleness, and self-control. Galatians 5:22-23

I had a dream I was carrying the Holy Chalice that is used for communion. The chalice is never touched by anyone except clergy but in this dream, I was lovingly holding the cup of salvation and feeling Christ's love.

Just as Bob and Mary's cups were filled with the love of God and given freely of the fruit of their lives and actions, so am I called to be full of abiding love of Christ and share His presence by giving the fruits of the Spirit from my cup and the platter of my life to all I meet.

Scripture says to give alms such as we have. Our lives are the alms we offer to God by loving our neighbors and sharing the fruits of the Spirit that we have. I believe this goes not for myself alone but all Christians.

Bob and Mary's cup and tray were filled to overflowing with love of God and His fruits. This book is filled with examples of this love that they offered their godchildren, family, friends, neighbors, and strangers. They gave freely of that love to all they encountered. Their joy in Christ was there and shared even in times of intense sorrow and banished bitterness with love, leaving joy, mercy, and empathy.

They were at peace and gave peace because they let God fill them with His Spirit and others through them with the fruits of the Spirit. They were patient and not easily offended because they knew the image of God was in every person they met.

Kindness and goodness were hallmarks of Bob and Mary. It was their natural language and in every action. Faithfulness to God never wavered no matter what the test. Harshness was not evident in their demeanor, only gentleness and self-control whose source was Christ.

As a cupbearer of Christ, my cup may not be full at times, and the gifts of the Spirit on the board of my life may be sparse. However, if I want to be clean and walk with God, I must share what I have.

I am called to offer the gifts I have no matter if it is a widow's mite. What matters is to begin to offer from what is in my cup and board, and the more I do this, the more I will be able to give to others. In doing this I love God and my neighbor as we share in His communion of grace; we are both clean and filled with His presence and renewed.

How this is done is only limited by the imagination. When I smile at someone on the street, show mercy, bring cookies to our neighbor, practice hospitality, greet a passerby, be pleasant to those who are tough to be with and really listen to someone who needs to talk. I know I am not alone in being able to do this. One never knows when one is entertaining angels.

Matthew 25 offers a list of opportunities such as feeding the hungry, giving a drink to a thirsty person, visiting the sick, welcoming a stranger, for whoever has done it to the least of us has done it to Christ.

Bob and Mary did this, and I believe it is possible for all to as well. Their lives illumined everyone they met; so can ours. Their lives appeared ordinary, as do ours, but were extraordinary; so can ours be if we walk in union with Christ and love our neighbor.

I saw this during those precious twenty years with Bob and Mary, and I know it is possible.

Married Life

I met my wife in 1998 while she was the married mother of three children at Saint Paul Orthodox Church in Las Vegas, Nevada. I became infatuated with her, and realizing that this was inappropriate, I transferred to Saint John Greek Orthodox Church in Las Vegas to avoid temptation.

I met her again at the church I was attending in 2012 and learned she had been divorced four years. We married a year later and I gained three wonderful stepsons who have been a joy to me ever since.

2013 *2023*

My wife was in the midst with others founding a new Orthodox Church that would serve the Russian Community in Las Vegas, and I was swept along. Services began in a local mortuary and later a storefront.

Kursk Root Icon

Olga and I along with many others were privileged by the visit of the Kursk Root Icon in 2013 and 2014. The icon was found under the root of a tree. Many years later an attempt was made to destroy it by cutting it in half and throwing the pieces aside. A priest found the pieces and put them together and the icon healed itself.

When revolution rocked Russia, the icon was removed from Russia and found its way over time to the United States. Millions of people throughout the world have been blessed by it and diseases cured.

Over its 700 hundred years of history, it healed Saint Seraphim of Sarov.

Saint John of Shanghai carried the icon to patients in hospitals and on his last trip to Seattle, reposed while in its presence.

She blessed our simple chapel twice. The first in 2014 when we had just moved into our store front and the second in 2015 when it looked like a church. Father Nicholas, now Metropolitan Nicholas, was the caretaker of the icon, and we were so thrilled to have seen and spent time with Her twice.

Eventually we moved to a larger property. In Her kindness she blessed Olga and me. We began our married lives having the opportunity to be in Her presence.

Until recently I did not realize how important meeting Her was. Marriage is hard work, and I believe only if God is in it can it be healthy and survive the tumult of daily life.

Man tried to destroy the icon, and God put it back together again. The enemy the devil will try to destroy a marriage, but if we ask God with humility and love He will always put it back together and heal it. Olga and I hang onto this.

I also realized that in a small way, Olga and I helped build a church much like Bob and Mary. We each have different gifts and talents, and God uses them for His glory.

Then Father Nicholas brought the icon to us in 2014. This is the chapel on Mojave before renovation.

Below are photos of Bishop Nicholas after renovation of the Chapel.

Our Rector Bishop Nikolai and then Bishop Nicholas, now Metropolitan of ROCOR

Bishop Nicholas speaking before the Holy

My Dear Wife Olga receiving Bishop Nikolas' Blessing Icon

Prayer

Over time we learned to pray together. We use a common prayer book but alternate with each other, one praying in English and the other in Russian.

On Sundays we pray the prayers of preparation to receive communion. When I take her to work, she will say the Morning Prayers as I drive. I continue my rule of prayer and reading when I come back home and try to read the Sixth Hour at Noon.

Ideal and Goal

My healing has not canceled my ego, and I discover new layers of selfishness daily which can only be overcome remembering the cross. Please God, more of thee and less of me.

Is drinking the poison of my ego worth indulging in the negative thoughts about my wife or others? Thoughts are seeds of either positive or negative action. Do I want those seeds to become actions that could harm my wife or bless her?

Are my thoughts greater than God's love, and the gift He gave me in my wife? Lord Jesus Christ have mercy on me and help me to have mercy on her as you have had mercy on me. This is not just in married life but in all relationships.

Failure and Cure

However, I fail, and my wife and I fight and argue occasionally. The strategy we employ is to first stop the emotional bleeding and treat the wounds inflicted by harsh words, then regroup and take time to be quiet and pray. When we are calmer, we admit wrong, and ask forgiveness of each other.

We ensure that we do this before we go to bed. If there is a Vespers or Vigil, we make sure to attend and go to confession to get the poison out of our souls and prepare ourselves to receive the Eucharist as soon as possible. In this way we can be touched by Christ and touch Him and be healed of the wounds we inflicted on each other.

Support of My Wife

I support my wife full time by taking care of her. This includes the running of the house. I look at everything as an opportunity to love God; by loving and honoring her, I honor Him who gave her to me.

It means like Bob I strive to take care of our home. When something breaks down or stops working, like him, I find a way with God's help to fix it.

She works twelve-hour shifts at a local hospital, and it is the least I can do. She has told me about her work, and I admire her for the love she has in doing it. When I am tempted to slide into the attitude that I do all the work in the house I snap myself back to reality. Her work is so much harder than the light work I do, and I have an opportunity to be a blessing to her in doing it.

Bob discovered long ago every time he did something for Mary, he loved her more and she him. The same is true with me when I am right in mind, heart, and spirit. Every time I bring her coffee in the morning, take her to work, clean the house or paint a room I love her more, and it is a gift and joy to do.

Life in Christ

In 2020 I retired from the military after twenty-two years of service. In 2022 I retired from the Clark County School District after twenty-five years of teaching grades first and third. I began to read about the Optima Elders, and this led to further reading about the Saints of the Orthodox Church.

I found that my identity as a soldier and teacher have become irrelevant to my present life replaced by the example of Bob and Mary. They focused on the eternal by living it in the present. That is my focus: seeking to live in freedom and union with Christ by doing the will of God that is found in the person in front of me.

I am no longer afraid to live, and I strive to love God and my neighbor by living as Bob and Mary in faith and love in daily life.

The miracle did not immunize me from the realities of daily life.
Sin distorts the original image of God that we were created to be and only as sin is resisted through prayer, humility, and love can one see the other as God sees them and as they truly are. It is not easy and can be done only with Christ's help.

We live in a world where there are a multitude of causes to be angry, to strike out from bunkers of self-righteousness, anger, self-pity, to not forgive because it is considered a weakness, to not apologize because one is always right.

It is a very comfortable box. The only thing that matters is one's emotions and self without regard to others. This box is toxic and deadly because those in it give the devil power to destroy and harm others.

It is dangerous to inhabit this small universe of self-absorption where one thinks they possess "godlike" powers, which is the pride of the former light-bearing angel Lucifer. This sin caused him to be cast out of Heaven like lightning, no longer illumined or bearing the light of God but the darkness of his own hellish pride.

In this box one strikes out with weaponized words more harmful than cigarette butts because fired from a sling shot of self-absorption are the stones of ego, anger, rage, malice, and hurt pride. Nothing good comes, just evil that destroys with fighting, strife, and cruelty leaving wounds in their wake lasting a lifetime.

I constantly need to resist and not allow myself to dwell in this box or use it to strike out at others.

C.S. Lewis offers some perspective in his essay titled, **The Trouble with X.** In it he writes that the people that surround us are called X.

X is the person who, if they changed, would make me or others happy. We notice and judge everything about them. The way they drive, their weight, their clothes, so much so that we do not notice ourselves and how we might annoy others.

God sees not only **X** but the person judging, and as bad **X** might be, so is the person judging. The person judging does not see their own faults and sins because they are focused on others and, unknown to him, is an **X** too.

Even if things were perfect, "real happiness would depend on the character of the people you have to live with." **The Trouble with X, CS Lewis, 1948, p. 2**

It begins to dawn on the judge that they are not God and cannot change others into their image.

What is more, God cannot either. He can if they allow Him to, but God has given free will to man. What is one to do?

The only way out is humility and to stay in union with Christ and realize others think the same about me. To realize I have caused people harm with my thoughts, words, and deeds and have been responsible for another's distress in what I have done or failed to. I am not a god, and when I sin and judge others I am more like a demon. This thought should drive me to my knees in repentance.

In this case repentance is turning away from judgment and reflecting on this quote by Lewis:

Every vile thought within our minds and yours, every moment of the spite, envy, arrogance, greed, and self-conceit comes right up against His patient and longing love and grieves His Spirit more than it grieves ours. **The Trouble with X, p. 3-4**

To repent means to turn away and to go from something bad and turn to something good. In this case turning from judging others and focusing on my sins, passions, and faults and repenting of them by turning to God. There is plenty I need to repent of while striving to follow Him while resisting the darkness of ego and pride. It requires carrying the cross of self-denial. Lord Jesus more of thee and less of me.

Praying for those I am in disharmony with redirects my mind to begin to see them as they are and not through the lens of my judgments, which are inaccurate and based on the faulty perceptions tinged by pride or envy.

Mary began to pray for Penny, and the cross became a bridge to her. On this bridge she denied her own pain and began to see Penny as someone who had led a tortured painful life. This created mercy, compassion, empathy, and love which was a path out of the turmoil in Mary's soul and allowed her to love and be present with her.

It is hard and difficult to turn from the self. Ego is very satisfying, an addictive drug and a deadly poison which, if untreated, leads to spiritual death. The only cure is humility, repenting, judging myself and loving my brothers and sisters through Him. This remains an ongoing work and will be complete only in Heaven.

When Bob was in the hospital for the final time a parishioner was with him, and he said Bob was struggling and asking what this was all about. He grasped the phrase, "Love trumps all." Love for God in sending his Son for us, love for each other, love of self, and love of neighbor is the only thing that can overcome the temptation of isolating oneself in the bunker of pride and striking out at others with judgment. Bob and Mary lived this love and showed how to overcome those temptations.

Inside All Saints Orthodox Church

In the next section I discuss cleaning the Holy Altar area. I would like to offer a brief view to acclimate those who are not familiar with this area.

Brief Explanation of the Parts of an Orthodox Church

When I clean the altar, I focus on two areas. The first area is behind the Royal Doors.

Iconostasis and Royal Doors

Royal Doors

Examples of areas I clean

Before   *After*

Before   *After*

This is called the Sanctuary and contains the Holy Altar and is the holiest place in church. I clean the sanctuary. I do not touch the altar.

The altar is located directly behind the iconostasis.

. 133 .

Cleaned Ambo

The next area is the Ambo the Deacon will read the Gospel and Litanies. Communion is also distributed here.

Nave of the Church

To provide some perspective this is a picture taken from the back of the Nave. The Nave is where the people of God worship. Here one can see the Iconostasis, the Royal Doors, and the Ambo.

Directly behind the Royal Doors is the Holy Altar. Only the Bishop, Priest, and Deacon may touch or stand behind the altar.

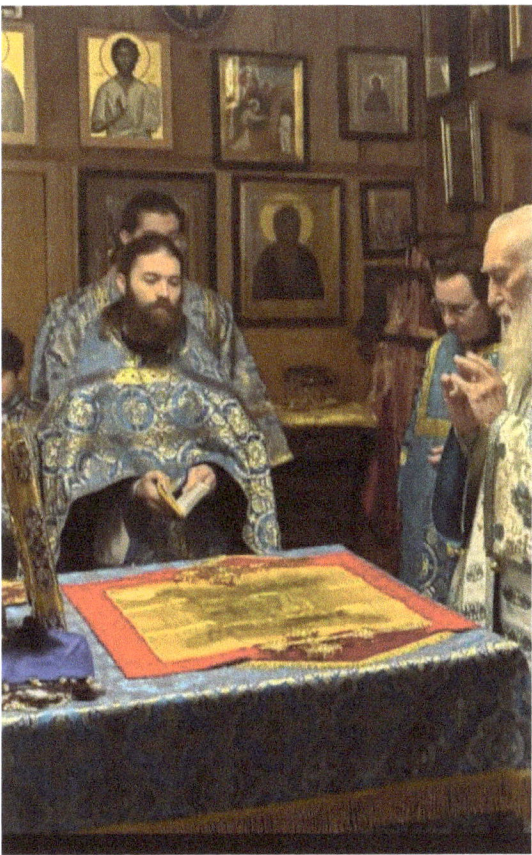

Father Dmitry, Deacon Thomas, and Bishop Nikolai at the Holy Altar.

Hierarchical Divine Liturgy Bishop Nikolai, Deacon Thomas
Priest Dmitri prepares to distribute Holy Communion. They are standing on The Ambo.
Bishop Nikolai is in front of the Royal Doors. Deacon Thomas is holding the Holy Chalice.
Father Dimitri is ready to distribute Holy Communion After the Prayer before Communion.

Church Life

My service in the church has evolved over time. I have served on the parish council, an altar server, and now sing in choir and clean the altar.

I served as an altar server and found that I was not good at it and developed a bad case of pride and stepped back from serving. It was an uncomfortable period.

I love singing, and over time the music has become part of me. Every song is a prayer to God when we are singing; there is a saying that when we sing, we pray twice.

Some examples are Lord, have mercy for the petitions offered on behalf of us and for us, prayers for the peace of the world, the creed, which is what we as a church believe, the songs for the feast of the day, and the Lord's Prayer just before communion. The intention is to lift our hearts and minds to Lord in prayer and adoration.

School of Humility

CLEANING THE SANCTUARY

The sanctuary or the altar area is the most sacred space in an Orthodox Church. The Holy Liturgy takes place in this sacred precinct; it is the Throne Room of God with the Holy Altar as His Throne.

After I left serving with the blessing of our Bishop, I started to clean the altar. It was an ideal job to tame my pride.

The Orthodox Church is one of light, and a symbol of this is the use of beeswax candles. During the service wax is often spilled on the floor. Over time it becomes the color of the floor and nearly invisible, hardens, and is a challenge to clean.

There is no better treatment for pride than finding and cleaning wax off a floor with a heat gun in one hand and Clorox wipe in the other. When I was raw with pride or anger, I would go into the sanctuary and pray as I cleaned. Gradually it would ease and make room for the grace of God.

I grew to love cleaning the altar and putting it in order. I would clean the glass in the framed icons of the saints and pray to them for their help and blessing. Then dust the shelves where the service books are located.

I would continue to dust and remove wax and soot from the surfaces of the tables where they are stored. After would come the sweeping of the floors, and I'd vacuum the rugs as well as mop the floor.

While doing this I said the Jesus prayer, Lord Jesus Christ forgive me the sinner, or talk to the Lord about the pressing issue of the moment. Sometimes I was emotional. I know he understands what it is to be human, and he heard me.

It is a very physical task. It requires sitting on the floor with a heat gun over spots of wax or kneeling before a piece of furniture to get the dust and dirt underneath.

Then to stand while vacuuming or mopping. I lift the heavy candle and incense holders to move them from place to place as I clean. All these are positions of prayer combined with work. Prayer and work are a form of worship and linked here as they are in daily life.

In prayer and work Bob and Mary worshipped God with their work in the church, and in taking care of their home and sharing it with others through the gift of hospitality.

As I focus on these tasks, I forget about myself and the pride that is replaced by God's peace and love.

I feel that I have done something worth doing. In this Holy Space Christ, the King, comes to be present with us in the Holy Chalice during Holy Communion.

After the liturgy He is present in the Tabernacle on the altar where the Reserved Sacrament is located. The King of All deserves an orderly and clean throne room. It is the least that can be done for Him, and I am honored and grateful to perform this task.

I am getting older. At sixty-one my legs get stiff, my joints occasionally pop, my hips hurt, and after six hours of cleaning I am exhausted. I found that I realized I am going to need help and invite others to help. I know I cannot continue to do it alone, and I need help and other people. This was a realization.

Isn't it better to invite others into the fellowship of the task and to learn from each other and enjoy each other's company while doing this work? Like Bob I invited my godson to help me with this work, and he has promised to do so.

We are going to invite the altar servers and others who want to help clean the sanctuary. The iconostases have not been cleaned since they were installed ten years ago and are due for a cleaning. We hope to make them shine and be a beacon of grace and beauty and draw people to the love of God.

In the cleaning of the altar God cleansed me of my pride and my overwhelming need to be somebody. This emphasis on self blinded me to the reality of who I belong to and who we are in Him and that I need other people as well.

The Warmth of Christ

In an email dated August 22, 2015, Mary conveyed the exciting news that Subdeacon Jeremiah was ordained to the Holy Diaconate. A short time later, he was ordained to the Holy Priesthood and, upon the retirement of Father James Bernstein, became the priest of Saint Paul the Apostle Orthodox Church in Brier, Washington. I was listening to his sermon one Sunday and thought it was a perfect way to end this work.

In the name of the Father, and of the Son, and of the Holy Spirit One God. Amen.

When the sun's rays touch a rock, the rock begins to shine. When a flame touches an unlit candle, it begins to burn. When a magnet touches a metal object, the object becomes magnetized. When an electric wire touches an ordinary wire, they both become electrified.

As we walk with God, we draw near to God; he draws near to us and changes us.

All these physical phenomena are only an image, or parable, of spiritual phenomena. All that takes place on the external plane is only an image of what happens on the internal plane. The whole of ephemeral nature is like a dream in relation to internal consciousness, and like a fairytale in terms of intransitory reality. The soul is the consciousness of the body, and God is the consciousness of the soul. When God touches the soul, it is vivified and given sight; when the soul touches the body, it does the same thing. The body receives light, warmth, magnetism and electricity, sight and hearing an movement from the soul. (St. Nikolai Velimirovich, Homilies, Vol. II, pg. 243)

As God draws near and with our permission he touches our soul, and it receives light, warmth, magnetism, electricity, sight, and hearing. The warmth and light I sought all my life I found by walking the pilgrimage to Christ with Bob and Mary.

Beloved, we become conformed to that which we prioritize in our lives. We truly do become whatever we unite ourselves to. Whatever it is we "plug into," this is what we become. We are contingent beings, we have no life in and of ourselves, we are needful.

I was plugged into my own box without Christ and isolated in my mind. I needed Christ and my godparent's. Now I need to stay connected to God, the Church, and others by loving them more than myself.

This is important for us to realize. We are in need. But, this is not the same as having the freedom to say "I need," which often means, "I desire," and we're not only formed by what we see, but defined by *how we see*.

Think about this phrase: "*I need to see Jesus.*" Consider those contemporaries who heard of this man, Jesus, simple, wise, dignified, unpredictable, exceedingly loving, yet a rock upon which hypocrisy shatters, accused by the powers-that-be, performing miracles at nearly every turn.

Wow, had I lived in Jerusalem and heard of such a man, I might say to myself "*I need to see Him, I need to see Jesus.*" This very well may be the case of the crowds we hear of, thronging about, pushing in upon the man who was a sight to behold, a spectacle to those who *"needed to see Him."* Yet, though even bumping against him and his disciples, they did not *really* touch Him, nor were they touched by Him. **They, perhaps, went forth shining the light of curiosity upon this enigma; yet a light that produces its own radiance blinds itself, and only projects itself outward, seeing only that which it "needs"—or really "wants"—to see.**

I had bumped into Christ in my wandering pilgrimage through different faith groups, but never was really touched by him until I entered the Orthodox Church, walked with them, and experienced first the communion of grace in them and in Him in Holy Communion.

What an incredible contrast we behold in the one who, in her illness, was not even seen as worthy to be in the midst of the crowd; due to her constant affliction she would have been considered unclean. The light of the curious and inquisitive ones (everyone else) would have quickly turned away from such person. *Perhaps she was afflicted by God, rejected because of some sin she committed*; **maybe we will look at her only enough to provide our own diagnosis, to cast our own judgment and attribute it to the Righteous Judge who hasn't judged** *me* **with such afflictions (or . . . maybe I'm more gifted at veiling mine).**

Back to the woman . . . I imagine her in a moment saying those same words as the others: "*I need to see Jesus*" and maybe even "I *need to touch Him.*" But as one so keenly aware of her own brokenness and unworthiness, having no light of curiosity to shine upon Him (for idle curiosity is the convenience of the unbroken—or of those who hide their brokenness), no need to 'spectate,' she realizes, "*I need not to see, but to be seen,*" not to touch, but to be touched.

My life was one of not being seen and my center a jumble of broken pieces like my stepfather. I needed to be seen, touched, healed, and remade by Christ. Bob and Mary helped that to happen. They lived the love of God and were able to convey it to me. I then became healed. When one is seen by God and touched by Him the real meaning of everything becomes apparent.

How we are viewed in this life, how much money we make, our physical appearance, our social status, none of it matters. What matters is that we love God and our brother and sister and try to see them as they are seen by God.

I am lost and bewildered, not finding my home in this word of spectators . . . in fact, I'm not worthy even to be touched, but if I can extend my hand to touch even the hem of His garment, it will suffice. Oh, to breathe the same air as the incarnate God is a gift in and of itself, let alone to touch His raiment. I may or may not be healed, but I will have come into contact with God.

In those twenty years of pilgrimage in the persons of Bob and Mary acting as God's hand, unworthy and broken as I was, I was touched by God. Through them I came to the church and in contact with God, and the shattered pieces both dark and the light were illumined and changed and set aright and transformed.

And then . . . in her humility she touched the untouchable one and power went forth! The others had their source, their reason and purpose, she was looking for hers and so His power went forth into her—His

uncreated energy—into the being who truly needed Him. Unoccupied with anything else, broken and desperate, undistracted, nothing left but the tears in her eyes and resounding rejection.

"Daughter, your faith has made you well."

In 2012 the warmth and light of God washed over me. The broken pieces became light, banishing the darkness and illumining the image of God that had been buried in fear. I was changed, healed, renewed. Son, your faith has made you well.

The untouchable one who touched the uncontainable God drew into herself what is proper to each creature; to be animated by the life that God gives—energized not by fleeting curiosity, the vain pursuits that seem so interesting at the time, then less so once the next big thing hits the news—to be animated by God's grace to be called "*daughter,*" and "*son*," by the Lover of mankind; this is the destiny of all who would become electrified by the unassuming power of the one who heals in the way that He knows how.

The pilgrim has met his Master. Walking with Bob and Mary, receiving Holy Communion, Confessing, and calling on the sweet name of Jesus as well as the prayers of Bob and Mary, I too became a son of God. This is God's call to all and for all. This is the life that Bob and Mary lived and their legacy.

It may be asked why so late, why this didn't happen earlier. I would answer, thank God it happened, and thank God for His timing. I am now sixty-one, a year short of Bob's age upon retirement. I am in the youth of my relationship with God, and I pray that I will walk as well as Bob and Mary in their twenty-four years at Saint Paul's for whatever time I have left. It is never too late to begin the journey.

She was healed of her physical ailments, as were many others, but not all.

But . . .

Behold what manner of love the Father has bestowed on us, that we should be called children of God! . . . Beloved, now we are children of God; and it has not yet been revealed what we shall be, but we know that when He is revealed, we shall be like Him, for we shall see Him as He is. And everyone who has this hope in Him purifies himself, just as He is pure. (1 Jn. 3:1-3)

Surely . . .

"When the sun's rays touch a rock, the rock begins to shine. When a flame touches an unlit candle, it begins to burn. When a magnet touches a metal object, the object becomes magnetized. When an electric wire touches an ordinary wire, they both become electrified."

But, when the human person stands before the Lord—the God of all creation—**as one who has none other help, she becomes transformed by grace ("*your faith has made you well*"), becoming, most truly, what she already is, a child of the living God.**

Beloved ones, this is our purpose and our true calling, to be the children of God—brought back to life by His grace—this is our healing and makes all that we face worthwhile.

This is our true purpose, to be children of God. All the darkness I went through was worth it to live in the warmth of God and living that life in the center of my being.

We have entered a slumber in our fallen state, and we're even tempted to return to it, yet we hear the voice of the Savior say to us, too: "*Child, arise!*" Let us not pretend to be asleep, or return to that slumber but let us arise as children of the most High, Sons and Daughters of the living God—who gives Himself to us freely, should we allow His light to shine upon us.

This pilgrimage is not over until life ends, and it is a continuous walk carrying the cross the Christ gives, but we know from scripture that the cross is light, and His grace makes it even easier to carry.

May He who bent low in a manner past telling continually make us His own as we work out our faith with fear and trembling; may God, our Father, be glorified in our lives, always, now and ever, and unto ages of ages. Amen.

The journey to live the life of Christ is one of letting go of the self and to love God and others more than self. It can only be done through the grace of God, through humility, love of neighbor and the sacraments of the Orthodox Church. It is not a battle that is won on one's own but with Christ and each other. Nor is it won in a single day but in each day of our lives in joys and sorrows, in the mundane daily reality of life, until our days are finished and we are with Him and each other in Heaven.

Icon written by the hand of Kimberly Mattson

Saint John of San Francisco describes holiness and in doing so perfectly describes Bob and Mary.

Holiness is not simply Righteousness, for which the righteous merit the enjoyment of blessedness in the Kingdom of God, but rather such a height of righteousness that men are filled with the grace of God to the extent that it flows from them upon those who associate with them. Great is their blessedness; it proceeds from personal experience of the Glory of God, they are responsive to men's needs, and upon their supplication appear also as intercessors and defenders for them before God. Christ the Savior-Holy Spirit Orthodox Church, A Living Proof of the Burning Faith: On St. John of Shanghai and San Francisco, Natalya Mihailova, 2 July 2014, Pramvir.com, Orthodox Christianity and the world, https://www.pravmir.com

Now is always the right moment to change, to become, to grow, to love as He loves us.

Listening to God

Miss Bacon said, **"If we listen, we can hear God's voice."** God speaks in many ways and with many voices but with one message, "I have come that they may have life, and have it abundantly." John 10:10

This book is full of voices that God spoke through. He speaks through the lives of those who love us, those we admire, through scripture, and the lives of the saints. He speaks to us through the Holy Liturgy, and the worship of the Church.

He speaks in a whisper when our minds are quiet from the tumult of noise that distracts us from Him and in times of turmoil when the waves seemingly will engulf us. He is speaking in our apparently everyday mundane life. Let us follow Miss Bacon's advice and try to listen for His voice so we can hear God and follow Him. In doing so we will live in Him. Then our lives and our neighbors' lives will be full of abundant life, light, grace, and the love of God and each other, and that is never mundane!

Let your light so shine before others, so that they may see your good works and give glory to your Father in Heaven (Matthew 5:16)

May the light of Christ illumine us all! As Mary so often said, Glory to God for all things!

Bibliography

Akrotirianakis, Stavros, Rev. *The Divine Fellowship of Holy Communion*, August 13, 2021, OCN, myocn.net.

Armstrong, Mary Vaughn, *Caregiving for Your Loved Ones*, David C. Cook Co., Elgin, Illinois, Weston, Ohio, 1990.

Armstrong, Mary Vaughn, *Quiet Moments for Parents and Other Caregivers*, David C. Cook Co., Elgin, Illinois, Weston, Ohio, 1992.

Athanasius, *On the Incarnation*, St. Vladimir's Seminary Press, Crestwood, NY, 2003.

Bloom, Anthony, *Beginning to Pray*, Paulist Press, Mahwah, NJ, 1982.

Bobrinsloy, Boris, "The one who prays is a theologian; the one who is a theologian, prays," Prayer, Spirituality, The Compassion of the Father, Theology, https://avowofconversation.wordpress.com/2010/07/27/"the-one-who-prays-is-a-theologian-the-one-who-is-a-theologian-prays-"/.

Catena Bible and Commentaries, http://catenabible.com, Quote of the Day, November 12, 2023, Saint Nectarios of Aegina.

Fagerberg, David, Note from Evagrius Ponticus: "If you truly pray you are a theologian," First Thoughts, http://cnn.com, February 4, 2019.

Goddard, John, Interviews with author and scrapbook prepared by Mary Goddard.

LeMaster, Philip, "Born to Raise the Image that Had Fallen: Homily for the Sunday Before Christmas in the Orthodox Church," https://easternchristianinsights.blogspot.com/2017/12/born-to-raise-image-that-had-fallen.html.

Lennox, John, *Why I Believe in God*, interviewed by Dr. Amy Orr-Ewing, 20 October 2023.

Lewis, C. S. The Trouble with X, The Church Union, Church Literature Association, 6 Hyde Park Gate, S.W. 7, circ 1948

Lewis, C.S. "The Weight of Glory," a sermon in the church of Saint Mary the Virgin, Oxford, June 8, 1942.

Mihailova, Natalya, "A Living Proof of the Burning Faith: On St. John of Shanghai and San Francisco," 2 July 2014, Pramvir.com, Orthodox Christianity and the world, https://www.pravmir.com

McGinnis, Jacob, Interview of Robert Armstrong, 2010-2011 and pictures of the Armstrongs.

Nieuwsma, Virginia, *Our Hearts' True Home*, Conciliar Press, Ben Lomand, California, 1996.

Orthodox Church of America Website, Volume 4: Spirituality, The Virtues, Hope, oca.org.

Orthodox Church Quotes, Saint Nectarios of Aegina, December 26, 2023, https://www.orthodoxchurchquotes.com/2013/07/25/st-nectarios-of-aegina-we-have-within-us-deeply-rooted-weaknesses-passions-and-defects/.

Pevear, Richard, and Volokhonsky, Larisa (translators), Preface by Olivier Clement, *Mother Maria Skobtskova, Essential Writings*, Orbis Books, Maryknoll, NY, 2003

Rose, Seraphim, *God's Revelation to the Human Heart*, St. Herman of Alaska Press, Platina, California, 1987.

Rozhneva, Olga, and Lukiano, Nicholai, *An Altar Server of St. John of Shanghai*, Publisher, City, Year. https://orthodchristian.com, Olga Rozneva, Nicholai Lukianov, Pravoslacie.ru, 7/2/2018.

Shakespeare, William, *Hamlet* I, iii, 55-81, readwritethink.org.

Further Reading

Mary Armstrong's books can be obtained through eBay and Amazon. They were published in the 1990s, but they are still applicable because human nature, sin, pain, and suffering are still present and have not changed. Neither has God's grace. The advice in these books is timeless in that it provides a path on how to overcome.

Virginia Nieuwsma's book, **Our Hearts' True Home**, edited and compiled by Virginia Nieuwsma, is a collection of the essays from fourteen accomplished women who converted to Orthodoxy. Their rich insights and wisdom are timeless and relevant.

Beginning to Pray by Anthony Bloom is a classic. It has been around since the 1960s and was the first book I read when I was starting to become interested in Orthodoxy.

God's Revelation to the Human Heart by Seraphim Rose is a brilliant, short, accessible book that can be read in a day. One of my favorite lines is, "The truly Orthodox person always has both feet firmly on the ground, facing whatever situation is right in front of him. It is in accepting given situations, which requires a loving heart, that one encounters God" (25). It is well worth the time spent to read it.

The Struggle for Virtue: Ascetism in a Modern Secular Society **by** Archbishop Averky. This is a superb book that lays out clearly the role that pride and the absence of God has played in our personal lives and culture. It is superb, readable, and reasoned, and answers the question why is our world this way and how can I live the life that I was intended to live and how to live it.

C.S. Lewis's *Christian Behavior.* I could not read C. S. Lewis's works other than the Narnia series until I was sixty-one. As the reader can probably tell, I am a late bloomer, and this applies to my appreciation of Lewis's writing. *Christian Behavior* is perfect for the busy person. It is short, cogent, and keeps the reader engaged on what the Christian life looks like. God speaks to us in many ways, and one of them is through reading great books. This is a great one, and I would highly recommend it.

Printed in the USA
CPSIA information can be obtained
at www.ICGtesting.com
CBHW061300110724
11388CB00012BA/168